Capital Punishment
The Death Penalty Debate

Capital Punishment
The Death Penalty Debate

Ted Gottfried

—Issues in Focus—

Enslow Publishers, Inc.

44 Fadem Road	PO Box 38
Box 699	Aldershot
Springfield, NJ 07081	Hants GU12 6BP
USA	UK

For Kourtney Guitierrez
—Peace and Love

Library of Congress Cataloging-in-Publication Data

Gottfried, Ted.
    Capital punishment : the death penalty debate / Ted Gottfried.
        p. cm. — (Issues in focus)
    Includes bibliographical references and index.
    Summary: Discusses the controversial issue of whether the death penalty is a
fair punishment, debating both sides of the argument.
    ISBN 0-89490-899-5
    1. Capital punishment—United States—Juvenile literature.
[1. Capital punishment.] I. Title. II. Series: Issues in focus (Hillside, N.J.)
KF9227.C2G68 1997
345.73'0773—dc20
[347.305773]   96-22719
                                          CIP
                                          AC

Printed in the United States of America

10 9 8 7 6 5 4 3 2

Illustration Credits: Amnesty International, p. 66; Collection of the New
York Public Library, pp. 14, 16, 95; Collection du Cabinet des Estamps, p. 98;
International Portrait Gallery, Collection of the New York Public Library,
pp. 19, 21; The Library of Congress, pp. 59, 88, 103; National Archives, pp.
23, 25, 100; National Coalition to Abolish the Death Penalty, pp. 11, 47,
54, 111; The office of Governor George Pataki, p. 79; The office of
Representative Bob Inglis, p. 42; The office of Senator Dale Volker, p. 33.

Cover Illustration: © TSM/Charles Gupton, 1993

Contents

Acknowledgments

I am deeply grateful to my friend Carl Sifakis, author of the *Encyclopedia of American Crime,* and to Steven Mundie of Amnesty International and Esther Green of the National Coalition to Abolish the Death Penalty for their help in assembling material for this book. As always, I am also indebted to those at the Mid-Manhattan branches of the New York Public Library as well as the Central Research Library and the central branch of the Queensboro Public Library.

I would like to acknowledge the never-failing support of my friend Janet Bode, and—with much love—the contribution of my wife, Harriet Gottfried, who—as always—read and critiqued each chapter of this book as it was written.

All contributed, but any shortcomings in the work are mine alone.

1

The Killer Who Wanted to Die

Should those who kill be executed by the state? Those who favor capital punishment say yes. Those who oppose it say no. Each side raises many other questions in arguing for or against the death penalty.

Does it prevent other murders, or does it cheapen life and make killing more likely? Is society served when murderers are allowed to live? What about wrongful executions? Does capital punishment insure that a murderer will never kill again? Are death sentences fairly imposed on rich and poor alike? On black and white? What about justice for victims and their families? Should those with low IQs be executed? Should children? Why should society pay to feed, clothe, and house a killer for life? Are all forms of execution uncivilized?

These are some of the questions raised. There are others. They are hard questions and not easily decided.

Yet the issue at the heart of them remains the same. Should society execute killers?

Are some crimes so terrible that only death will satisfy justice? If so, then surely the murders committed by Thomas Grasso are among them. He paid for his crimes on March 20, 1995, after two years of delays involving a headline-making struggle between two states over whether or not it was morally right to execute a murderer.

Two Brutal Murders

Grasso's story begins in Tulsa, Oklahoma, on Christmas Eve of 1990. He was twenty-eight years old when he forced his way into the home of a neighbor, Hilda Johnson, who was eighty-seven. Grasso demanded money, but Mrs. Johnson refused to give him any. There was a struggle that knocked over the elderly woman's Christmas tree. Grasso pulled out the electrical cord from the tree lights, wrapped it around Mrs. Johnson's neck, and strangled her. Then, seeing that she was still alive, he bashed her on the head with an electric iron. He struck her many times until he was sure that she was dead. The crime netted Grasso $12 in cash and $125 for the TV set he stole.

The killer fled Tulsa and went to New York City. Seven months later he was arrested there for another murder. He had strangled an old man, a neighbor. Grasso was convicted, sentenced to twenty years to life, and locked up in New York's Sing Sing prison.

At that time, New York had no death penalty. For sixteen years the state legislature had been passing capital punishment bills, and for sixteen years Governor Hugh Carey and then Governor Mario Cuomo had used their veto power to block passage by refusing to sign them into law. At the time of his 1984 veto, Governor Cuomo had declared, "I believe the death penalty demeans the values that form the core of American life." He added, "capital punishment is . . . a desperate response that substitutes one evil for another."[1] Since then, although it had been close more than once, his veto had always stood.

So Grasso, now thirty years old, faced spending the rest of his life in prison—except for one catch. When he was arrested in New York, he had also confessed to killing Mrs. Johnson in Oklahoma. Now Grasso was taken to Tulsa under the Interstate Agreement on Detainers, which allows prisoners to be transferred to another state to stand trial for other crimes. By the terms of this agreement, after the Tulsa trial, Grasso would be returned to New York to serve out his time there before any Oklahoma sentence could be carried out.

Life or Death

But Grasso wanted to die. He preferred death to life in prison. He pleaded guilty to murdering Mrs. Johnson and asked to be executed. The Oklahoma court sentenced him to death. Grasso asked that he not be returned to New York and that the Oklahoma sentence be carried out. If New York agreed, he would be executed.

New York, however, did not agree. The state demanded the return of its prisoner. Governor Mario Cuomo backed up that demand. He had said on many occasions that "there is a better response to killing than killing,"[2] and now he stood by his words.

There were legal moves and countermoves, but finally New York got its way. Grasso was returned to Sing Sing. Meanwhile the struggle between New York and Oklahoma had focused the nation's attention on capital punishment. Governor Cuomo was running for re-election, and the Grasso case along with Cuomo's vetoes of the death penalty became one of the major issues of the campaign. His opponent George Pataki announced that his first official act as governor would be to send Grasso back to Oklahoma to die.

Mario Cuomo lost the election. While there were other issues, his stand against the death penalty was certainly one of the major reasons for his defeat. The next time the New York State legislature passed a death penalty bill, the new governor George Pataki signed it into law, proclaiming a victory for justice.[3] Before voting for the bill, leading Democrat Sheldon Silver said that while capital punishment would not prevent any murders, it was what the people wanted and he was bowing to their will. By then Governor Pataki had returned Thomas Grasso to Oklahoma to die.

Last Words

The execution took place shortly after midnight on March 20, 1995. The method was lethal injection. It took about five minutes to legally execute Grasso. Once Grasso had been asked if he had any regrets. "I regret getting caught,"[4] he had answered. Immediately before

Mario Cuomo lost his position as governor of New York to George Pataki, partly due to his anti-death penalty stance.

his death, he wrote, "Cuomo is right. Life without parole is much worse than the death penalty."[5]

Shortly after the execution, Cuomo, now ex-governor, responded that Grasso "admitted that being allowed to die was an act of clemency for a double murderer, relieving him of the relentless confinement he dreaded more than death."[6]

Is that right? What do you think? Is it a harsher punishment to lock up murderers for life than to legally execute them?

2

History of the Death Penalty in the United States

Among the first people to be put to death for crimes in the colonies, which would one day become the United States of America, were so-called "witches."[1] One witch was hanged in Charlestown in 1648, another in Boston in 1655. But the best known are those whose lives were taken during the witchcraft trials in Salem, Massachusetts, between May and October of 1692.

It all began with ten young girls, aged nine to seventeen, and a West Indian slave named Tituba, who told them stories of magic spells and murder. One night one of the girls, a minister's daughter named Elizabeth Parris, awoke from a nightmare screaming and throwing around her body. She could not be quieted. A doctor examined her and said that she was under an evil spell. People of Salem spread the word that there was a witch among them.

Soon other children began throwing tantrums,

screaming and crying, shaking their bodies, and frothing at the mouth. They said that they too had been bewitched and they were believed. When asked who had cast evil spells over them, they named different people.

The citizens of Salem were good English folk who lived by the Bible and the law. The Bible read, "Thou shalt not suffer a witch to live."[2] English law stated that every person accused of a crime—even the crime of witchcraft—must have a trial. And so judges were selected, juries were picked, and trials were held.

When the trials were over, twenty people had been sentenced to die. One of them, an eighty-year-old man named Giles Corey, was pressed to death by piling weights on his chest. The other nineteen were hanged.

By that time, the people of Salem had come to doubt the charges that the young girls continued to make. Soon the judges and jurors who had been involved in the trials were saying that there had been a mistake and that the executions should not have taken place. The jurors signed a paper admitting that they had been "under the power of a strong and general delusion."[3]

English Law

Really they had followed English law, which is the basis of the laws of the United States today. Back then in England, and through much of the eighteenth century, death was the punishment for several hundred offenses. These included murder as well as witchcraft. But most of the crimes punishable by death were crimes against property rather than violence against people. Arson (barn-burning was a common form of revenge),

13

Many people were hanged as witches during the famous Salem withcraft trials in 1692.

pickpocketing, swindling, embezzlement, extortion, and robbery were all punishable by death under English law.

The ways in which the colonies followed English law varied. In Massachusetts, where the Salem witch trials were held, death remained the punishment for thirteen crimes until the American Revolution. In addition to witchcraft, these "crimes" included cursing, adultery, praying to false idols, lying under oath, and other more serious offenses such as rape, kidnapping, and murder. In Pennsylvania, however, the Great Act of 1682 stated that only treason and murder could be punished by death. And in the Quaker colony of South Jersey, capital punishment was not permitted for any crime. But most of the colonies had harsh laws that punished a wide variety of crimes by death.

The general opinion was that the harshness of these laws discouraged crime. This was also the view of almost all of the leaders of the American Revolution. They may have had different ideas about just which crimes, or how many, should be punished by death. Yet most of them believed that crime should be punished, and punished harshly, and that some crimes were so evil that those who committed them deserved to die.

Two who did not share this belief were the noted patriot Benjamin Franklin and the highly respected attorney general of Pennsylvania William Bradford. They had been influenced by Dr. Benjamin Rush, author of a pamphlet titled "Inquiry into the Justice and Policy of Punishing Murder by Death." Rush is considered to be the founder of the anti-capital punishment movement in the United States.

Benjamin Franklin, the famous inventor and scientist, did not believe in capital punishment.

Dr. Benjamin Rush

Dr. Rush was a most unusual person. He was born in Philadelphia in 1745 and lived there until his death in 1813. During his life, he was admired and respected as a doctor, scientist, writer, patriot, and reformer. At the time of his death, he was the treasurer of the United States.

Dr. Rush believed that the war to free the colonies from England should also "effect a revolution in our principles, opinions, and manners"[4] suited to a government of free and forward-looking citizens. He opposed slavery, thought women should be educated as men were, and spoke out for free public schools for all children. He worked with the mentally ill, and for years, his writings on mental illness were required reading for American psychiatrists.

When he became interested in crime, Rush looked at it as doctors look at sickness—an ailment to be cured. Because we do not cure an illness by killing the patient, Rush opposed capital punishment. At the same time he believed that crime—and the criminal—had to be *treated*. Since crime affected others, the criminal would have to be treated some place away from the rest of society.

Rush, with Franklin and Bradford's support, proposed a "House of Reform,"[5] a place away from others where criminals could be held while being taught to change their behavior. The result was the first United States prison. The Walnut Street Jail was built in Philadelphia in 1790. In effect, Rush had founded the American prison system.

Doing away with the death penalty was another

matter. Even with the support of his friend Benjamin Franklin, perhaps the most popular man in Philadelphia, Rush was fighting an uphill battle. He believed that the state of Pennsylvania—indeed all states—had no right to execute a citizen. He did not believe that killing a criminal prevented crime. "Thou shalt not kill"[6] was his answer to those who quoted the Bible as justification for the death penalty.

These views were even less popular then than they are now. Still Rush, Franklin, and Bradford were able to exert strong influence on the citizens and the lawmakers of Pennsylvania. As a result, it was decided that no crimes except first-degree murder should be punished by the death penalty in that state.

The movement to limit or end the death penalty spread. Groups opposing capital punishment formed in other states. Petitions were presented to lawmakers in Ohio, New Jersey, New York, and Massachusetts. None of them, however, succeeded in having the laws changed.

The First Conflicts

After Rush's death in 1813, many groups opposed to the death penalty continued to be formed, but the lack of a powerful spokesperson kept them from accomplishing much. Then, in the 1840s, that situation changed. Horace Greeley—founder and editor of the *New York Tribune*, possibly the most influential newspaper in the country—became a leader in the fight against the death penalty. In 1845, the American Society for the Abolition of Capital Punishment was founded. And in 1846, Michigan, a territory that was not yet a state, did away

Dr. Benjamin Rush was a vocal opponent of the death penalty.

with the death penalty entirely—replacing it with life imprisonment.

Michigan was the first place in the United States to stop using capital punishment. Rhode Island and Wisconsin followed. Before and during the Civil War, attention turned away from the question of the death penalty; but after the war, both Maine and Iowa passed laws ending capital punishment. Angry citizens objected, insisting that crime should be severely punished. The legislatures of both states reversed themselves and restored the death penalty. But in 1887, Maine again abolished capital punishment.

This back-and-forth pattern would be repeated. The opposing views it reflected were voiced by many spokespersons. Favoring the death penalty were philosopher and political economist John Stuart Mill in England and renowned attorney Samuel Hand in the United States. Among those who led the fight against the death penalty were Horace Greeley and railroad executive Robert Rantoul, Jr.

Hand believed that "capital execution" was "necessary for the safety of society."[7] Mill, a social reformer in most matters, was more concerned with the criminal. He thought that "the short pang of a rapid death" was a kinder punishment than "a long life in the hardest and most monotonous toil" in a prison, which was in reality "a living tomb."[8]

Answering Hand's argument, Rantoul insisted that "it is not necessary to hang the murderer in order to guard society against him, and to prevent him from repeating the crime."[9] Greeley did not want to involve himself in the argument over "whether Hanging or Imprisonment for Life is the severer penalty."[10] He was more concerned about the effects of capital punishment on the larger society—"the moral it teaches."[11] He felt that killing criminals, even murderers, sent the wrong message. "I feel," he wrote, "that the choking to death of this culprit works harm."[12] Among his reasons were that "it [capital punishment] teaches and sanctions Revenge"[13] and that "it tends to weaken and destroy the natural horror of bloodshed."[14]

The Law Changes—and Changes Back

The argument was continued in the United States Congress. After much debate, in the late 1880s, the federal government passed a law limiting the number of

Horace Greeley, the founder and editor of the *New York Tribune*, was an early leader in the fight to abolish the death penalty in the United States.

21

crimes punishable by death to three: treason, murder, and rape. This, and the example of states such as Michigan and Maine, influenced Colorado lawmakers to outlaw the death penalty. But Colorado citizens were so outraged by this act that they took the law into their own hands. Angry mobs dragged convicted murderers from the jails where they were being held and lynched them. The Colorado lawmakers brought back the death penalty.

In the early 1900s, with reform movements in many different areas gaining acceptance in the United States, anti-capital punishment forces had an effect on one state after another. Between 1907 and 1917, nine states plus Puerto Rico did away with the death penalty. However, as in the past, by 1921, five of these states had brought it back. This time those opposed to capital punishment did not quickly regain the ground that they had lost.

Still, during that period in the 1920s, there were leaders who spoke out against it. Among them were newspaper publisher William Randolph Hearst and famous defense attorney Clarence Darrow—unlikely allies since Darrow was a reformer on the political left and Hearst a conservative on the right. Hearst lectured that "we cannot cure murder by murder,"[15] while Darrow wrote that the main purpose of capital punishment was "to appease the mob's emotions of hatred and revenge."[16]

The men were answered by the highly respected Judge Robert E. Crowe, and by a 1925 editorial in the *Cleveland Plain Dealer*. Judge Crowe pointed out that "it is the finality of the death penalty which instills fear into the heart of every murderer, and it is this fear of punishment which protects society."[17] The *Plain Dealer* put it

The executions of Nicola Sacco (right) and Bartolomeo Vanzetti (center) caused a tremendous amount of national and international turmoil. Riots and demonstrations erupted worldwide in response to the possibility of trumped up charges against the two.

more bluntly: "If we want order, we must stop being soft-headed sentimentalists when it comes to penalizing offenders."[18] The editorial continued, "The murder rate in the United States rises to a scandalous figure."[19] Only the fear of "prompt and adequate punishment"[20] could reverse it, and that meant the death penalty.

Between 1917 and 1957, no new states abolished capital punishment. During that time only seven states out of forty-eight had no death penalties. Then, in the late 1950s, the territories of Alaska and Hawaii and the

23

state of Delaware discarded capital punishment. Three years later Delaware brought it back, but Oregon, Iowa, and West Virginia eliminated it and other states reduced the number of crimes punishable by death.

The Legal Seesaw

In 1967, a collection of anti-capital punishment groups brought a series of lawsuits—*Furman* v. *Georgia, Jackson* v. *Georgia, Branch* v. *Texas, Gregg* v. *Georgia, Proffitt* v. *Florida,* and *Jurek* v. *Texas*—that reached the United States Supreme Court. The vague wording of the decisions reached by the Court stopped states from enforcing death sentences for the next ten years. There were no executions anywhere in the United States between 1967 and 1977. In 1976, in another case, the Supreme Court ruled more clearly, deciding that the death penalty is constitutional. In 1977, the state of Utah executed the murderer Gary Gilmore by firing squad.

In the eighteen years since Gilmore's death—as of October 1995— there have been three hundred executions. Most of these have been in southern states, with Texas accounting for ninety-nine of them. In early 1995, under its new governor, George Pataki, New York became the thirty-eighth state to adopt capital punishment. At present there are twelve states that still do not have the death penalty. They are Alaska, Hawaii, Iowa, Maine, Massachusetts, Michigan, Minnesota, North Dakota, Rhode Island, Vermont, West Virginia, and Wisconsin. Nor does the District of Columbia (Washington, D.C.) have capital punishment.

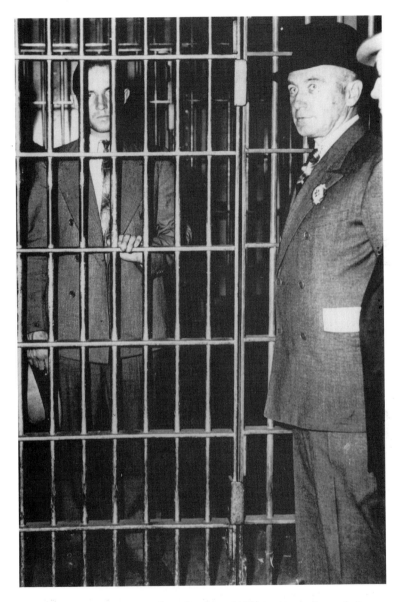

Bruno Hauptmann was found guilty of kidnapping and murdering the child of the famous aviator Charles Lindbergh. Even though some people doubted his guilt, he was executed for this crime.

Other Nations

In its use of the death penalty, the United States stands with the majority of the world's nations. Historically all nations—even those that today have abolished the death penalty—have embraced it for long periods of their history. Countries that are widely separated geographically and seemingly have very different cultures have all put people to death by various methods for various crimes. The crimes range from heresy—speech at odds with religious doctrine—to indecency—obscene speech or immodest dress—to cheating at cards to rape and murder and treason. Most of these nations have modified the number of crimes punishable by death, and many countries that have death penalty laws have not used them in many years.

The first nation to do away with capital punishment was Venezuela in 1863. Between 1976, when the Supreme Court restored the death penalty in the United States, and 1995, thirty-one nations ended the death penalty entirely and eleven countries did away with it for all crimes except those committed in exceptional circumstances, such as breaking military law or wartime offenses. Among those countries where capital punishment is permitted, twenty-eight of them have not executed anyone for ten years or more. Most recently, in June 1995, South Africa—under the government of Nelson Mandela—ended capital punishment.

Today most of the major industrialized nations of the world have abolished the death penalty. The United States, with the highest crime rate in the industrialized world, is one of the very few that executes criminals. On the other hand, countries such as Singapore, Sri Lanka, Argentina, and China, which strictly enforce the death penalty, report very low crime rates.

The following tables list those countries that do or do not have the death penalty.

Death Penalty Nations[21]

(These countries enforce the death penalty for ordinary crimes and most have carried out executions during the past ten years.)

Afghanistan	Botswana	Ethiopia
Albania	Bulgaria	Gabon
Algeria	Burkina Faso	Georgia
Antigua and Barbuda	Cameroon	Ghana
Armenia	Chad	Grenada
Azerbaijan	Chile	Guatemala
Bahamas	China	Guinea
Bangladesh	Cuba	Guyana
Barbados	Dominica	India
Belarus	Egypt	Indonesia
Belize	Equatorial Guinea	Iran
Benin	Eritrea	Iraq
Bosnia-Herzegovina	Estonia	Jamaica

Death Penalty Nations (cont'd)

Japan	Mongolia	Tadzhikistan
Jordan	Morocco	Taiwan
Kazahkstan	Myanmar	Tanzania
Kenya	Nigeria	Thailand
Korea (North)	Oman	Trinidad and Tobago
Korea (South)	Pakistan	Tunisia
Kuwait	Poland	Turmenistan
Kyrgyzstan	Qatar	Turkey
Laos	Russia	Uganda
Latvia	Saint Kitts-Nevis	Ukraine
Lebanon	Saint Lucia	United Arab Emirates
Lesotho	Saint Vincent and the Grenadines	United States
Liberia	Saudi Arabia	Uzbekistan
Libya	Sierra Leone	Vietnam
Lithuania	Singapore	Yemen
Malawi	Somalia	Yugoslavia
Malaysia	Sudan	Zaire
Mauritania	Swaziland	Zambia
Moldova	Syria	Zimbabwe

Non-Death Penalty Nations[22]

Andorra	Honduras	Norway
Angola	Hong Kong	Panama
Australia	Hungary	Portugal
Austria	Iceland	Romania
Cambodia	Ireland	San Marino
Cape Verde	Italy	São Tomé and Principe
Colombia	Kiribati	Slovak Republic
Costa Rica	Liechtenstein	Slovenia
Croatia	Luxembourg	Solomon Islands
Czech Republic	Macedonia	South Africa
Denmark	Marshall Islands	Sweden
Dominican Republic	Micronesia	Switzerland
Ecuador	Mauritius	Tuvalu
Finland	Monaco	Uruguay
France	Mozambique	Vanuatu
Germany	Namibia	Vatican City State
Greece	Netherlands	Venezuala
Guinea-Bissau	New Zealand	
Haiti	Nicaragua	

Non-Death Penalty Nations That Make Exceptions[23]

(These countries only use the death penalty in exceptional cases.)

COUNTRY	DATE OF LAST RECORDED EXECUTION
Argentina	Unknown
Brazil	1855
Canada	1962
Cyprus	1962
El Salvador	1973
Fiji	1964
Israel	1962
Malta	1943
Mexico	1937
Nepal	1979
Paraguay	1928
Peru	1979
Seychelles	Unknown
Spain	1975
United Kingdom (England, Scotland, Northern Ireland, and Wales)	1964

The United States is unusual in that it is the only country in the world where the law regarding the death penalty within its borders is not uniform. In no other country does it vary from state to state as in the United States, or for that matter from district to district, or area to area.

The Case for Punishment by Death

In 1976, in Albany, the state capital of New York, Lemuel Smith held up a store that sold religious materials. During the robbery, he killed both the owner of the store and an employee. In 1977, Smith kidnapped a Schenectady, New York, woman and robbed her. He was finally caught, tried, and convicted of the two earlier murders and the robbery-kidnapping. He was sentenced to three terms of twenty-five years to life in prison.

While in prison, Smith strangled Donna Payant, a corrections officer. After she was dead, he cut up her body. On April 21, 1983, Smith was convicted of her murder. He was then sentenced to die in the electric chair under a New York State law that called for capital punishment in the case of a murder by a person serving a life term in prison.

At this time, New York State had not executed anyone since August 1963. This was partly because of the

31

United States Supreme Court decision that cast doubt on the legality of all of the states' capital punishment laws. It was also partly because two successive New York governors—Hugh Carey and Mario Cuomo—had vetoed all attempts by successive New York state legislatures to write a death penalty law that would satisfy the Supreme Court.

However, the state law ruling that New York must execute anyone serving a life sentence who committed murder while in prison was still on the books. In 1977, the New York State Court of Appeals had refused to decide if the law was legal or not. Now the issue was raised again in connection with the death sentence of Lemuel Smith.

This time the New York State Court of Appeals agreed to hear the case. On July 2, 1984—more than a year after Smith was sentenced to die—the court ruled that the law did not hold up. The prosecution appealed the decision to the United State Supreme Court. On February 19, 1985, the Supreme Court upheld the state court ruling. As a result, Lemuel Smith could not be executed, and New York State was left without a death penalty law.

Getting Away with Murder

One person who was particularly outraged by this situation was Senator Dale M. Volker. Senator Volker, author of the death penalty bill that would be signed into law by Governor Pataki in 1995, had been seeking death penalty legislation since 1977. Most of his attempts to pass such a law had met with success in both the state

Senator Dale Volker drafted the death penalty bill that was signed by Governor Pataki in New York. Previous Governors Cuomo and Carey vetoed the bill.

senate and assembly, but there had never been enough votes in the assembly to override the vetoes by Governors Carey and Cuomo.

Governor Cuomo had suggested sentences of life without parole as an alternative to death sentences for convicted murderers. Yet if Lemuel Smith had been sentenced to death originally, say those who favor capital punishment, corrections officer Donna Payant would still be alive. Furthermore, other guards and inmates would not be in danger of being killed by Lemuel Smith as he lived out his life in prison.

Their point of view was summarized by the judge passing sentence in another case—that of Willie Boskett. In 1989, Boskett was tried and convicted for stabbing a guard while in prison. With no death penalty available, by law the judge had to sentence him to twenty-five years to life. But the judge was not happy. "I'm sure you are going to kill somebody," the judge told Boskett, "so in sentencing you, I'm inevitably sentencing an innocent man to death."[1]

The sentence of twenty-five years to life also allowed for parole. As long as the offender was alive, he was eligible for clemency. According to Bureau of Justice Statistics, among young adults convicted of murder and paroled in 1978, 6 percent were re-arrested for murder within six years of their release. Recent data may indicate that the figure has climbed much higher. The Justice Department's 1993 Crime Victimization Study shows that 10 percent of those on death row had a prior homicide conviction.

Governor Cuomo released Gary McGivern on New

Year's Eve in 1985. McGivern had been found guilty of murdering a Westchester County deputy sheriff. The Volker Bill, now New York State law, allows for the death penalty where "the intended victim was a police officer."[2] Under it, Gary McGivern might have been put to death rather than released to once again menace the community.

Killers Will Kill Again!

Thus, life imprisonment as opposed to death not only puts prison staffs and fellow prisoners at risk from those who have shown that they are willing to kill, but the ordinary citizen as well. People who kill will kill again. So say those who want capital punishment, and they offer the following evidence: Of those arrested for murder in New York City in 1975–1976, eighty-five had previously been arrested for killing. In New Jersey, Richard Biegenwald was released from prison after serving eighteen years for murder and killed four more people.

Execution, these people point out, stops the murderer before he or she can kill again. Between 1988 and 1993, 14 percent of death row inmates had received two or more death sentences. Indianapolis Police Chief Ed Davis puts it this way: "You don't shoot a rabid dog to deter other rabid dogs; you shoot him so he won't bite somebody."[3]

In fact, many who favor the death penalty do view it as a way of preventing future murders. They point to national and local crime statistics as proof of their claim. The FBI *Uniform Crime Reports* for 1993 shows that "while the Nation's homicide rate per 100,000 residents was 9.3 in 1992, the historical high actually occurred 13 years prior,"[4] when many states had not yet begun to enforce the death penalty. Once the death penalty began being enforced in earnest in states all across America, the murder rate decreased. Also, the report found that "The Nation's cities collectively recorded a 1-percent decrease"[5] in murders for 1993 over 1992. Most impressively, a later mid-year report showed that "the number of murders dropped 5 percent"[6]—more in 1994 as compared to 1993.

There is historic state evidence as well. In New York, between 1940 and 1965 when the death penalty was in effect, there were 12,652 murders. Between 1966 and 1991 when there were no executions, there were 51,638 murders—"*four times* the number of murders than occurred in the *same period of time* prior to the abolishment of capital punishment. On average there were less than 500 murder victims a year"[7] in New York when the state had the death penalty. During the years New York did not have it, 1993 marked *"the sixth straight year that more than 2,200 people have lost their lives"*[8] by murder.

Norman Darwick, executive director of the International Association of Chiefs of Police, is sure that "many potential murderers are deterred simply by their knowledge that capital punishment exists and it may be their fate if they commit the crime they contemplate."[9] Even some criminals agree. Luis Vera, who shot and killed Rosa Velez when she found him robbing her apartment, is one. "Yeah, I shot her," he confessed. "She knew me, and I knew I wouldn't go to the chair."[10]

"Retribution," Not Revenge

Such killers have no regard for life and deserve to die according to those who are for the death penalty. Jacob Sullum, who writes on capital punishment, uses the case of Robert Alton Harris to prove his point. "He killed his victims after telling them they would not be harmed, shooting one as he walked away and the other as he begged for mercy. Afterward, Harris laughed about the murders and finished the boys' lunches. Does such a man deserve to live?"[11] asks Sullum.

His answer is definitely no. To execute Harris, he writes, is not a matter of revenge, but rather "retribution, and therefore just and proper. . . . What distinguishes revenge from retribution," he adds, "is the motive. The execution of a murderer makes a statement. It says that people like Robert Alton Harris have committed a crime so grave that they have forfeited their right to live; it elevates human life even as it ends the killer's."[12]

A report by the Senate Committee on the Judiciary, which studied capital punishment, states that "people who commit violent crimes have forfeited their own right to life."[13] The committee concluded that the legal system must satisfy the righteous anger of ordinary, law-abiding citizens towards criminals who kill. Only stern enforcement of the death penalty, according to committee member Senator Strom Thurmond, can restore "the confidence of the American people in our criminal justice system."[14]

Some death penalty supporters regard murder as a violation of human rights. The question that they ask is if those who violate the rights of others should be given the opportunity to do so again? To them it is a significant moral question.

Others insist that it is because they believe in the sanctity of life that they are for it. Beyond the idea that punishment should be as harsh as the crime committed, they hold that the sanctity of life itself demands that when it is snuffed out, it be punished by death. They stress that life itself is cheapened when we do not punish people who commit murder more harshly than people who commit lesser crimes.

With a similar respect for life, death penalty supporters try to deal with the objections raised by those who are against capital punishment. Answering the argument that innocent people have been executed and that others may be, they agree that every precaution must be taken to insure that it does not happen. They insist that while it may have happened in the past, there are increasingly more safeguards in place to see that it cannot happen again.

The Death Penalty Prevents Murders

Yet they do not necessarily believe that it is better that the guilty should go free than that an innocent person should be killed. Some of those who favor capital punishment reason that the death penalty has prevented many uncounted murders. They point to the figures presented earlier in this chapter. They cannot give the number of killings prevented, but neither can the other side prove that the number is not large enough to justify a rare error, no matter how awful. It is the price that must be paid for having a society in which law and order prevail.

Professor Ernest van den Haag, teacher of public policy at Fordham University, puts it this way: "All human activities—building houses, driving a car, playing golf or football—cause innocent people to suffer wrongful death, but we don't give them up because on the whole we feel there's a net gain. Here [executions] a net gain in justice is being done."[15]

Supporters of the death penalty deny the charge that it is racist because there are so many more blacks than whites on death row compared to their numbers in the population. When Warren McCleskey, a black man, was convicted of murdering a white police officer, his lawyers appealed the verdict on the grounds that killers of whites were four times as likely to be sentenced to death in the state of Georgia as killers of blacks. The Supreme Court rejected the argument, pointing out that "apparent disparities in sentencing are an inevitable part of our criminal justice system."[16]

Racism Not a Factor

Carrying the Supreme Court's logic one step further, pro-capital punishment journalist Laurence W. Johnson considered the fact that "most murderers of blacks are themselves black."[17] Far from being an act of bigotry, ridding this community of these killers is making African Americans more safe and secure in their homes. Many African Americans support the death penalty for just that reason.

Backing up this support is the fact that 94 percent of

black murder victims are killed by blacks according to the FBI's 1993 *Uniform Crime Reports*. It is also worth noting that the Bureau of Justice Statistics for 1995 shows that whites convicted of murder spend thirteen months *less* time on death row than African Americans do. Death penalty supporters find little evidence to back up claims of discrimination against blacks in its administration.

Even so, the general feeling among death penalty supporters is that if race is a factor, every effort should be made to correct that injustice. But that no more means that we should do away with the death penalty than that we should do away with all police because of the few that are racist. The argument is the same when it comes to poor people and capital punishment.

When Senator Ted Kennedy called the death penalty "the ultimate discrimination against poor people,"[18] he was answered by Professor van den Haag, who believes that how fairly capital punishment is applied to African Americans and poor people is "wholly irrelevant."[19] Such charges look at "the unfair way in which the penalty is distributed, not the fairness or unfairness of the penalty"[20] itself. Professor van den Haag reasons that the wrong "is not in the penalty, but in the process."[21]

Jury selection is part of that process. Supporters believe that those who oppose the death penalty should be barred from serving on capital punishment juries because their bias will keep them from reaching a fair verdict. They also believe that the appeals process should be shortened so that those condemned to death cannot postpone their fate indefinitely. There are bills before both houses of Congress that could help to do that.

Reforming the Appeals Process

A rider to a recent appropriations bill eliminates funding for twenty law offices known as death penalty resource centers, which were financed by the federal government at a cost of roughly $20 million a year. The attorneys at these centers worked with death row prisoners to file appeals. However, according to South Carolina Attorney General Charlie Condon, "These lawyers have become lobbyists whose only goal is to stop executions at any cost."[22] His view is shared by many state attorney generals, district attorneys, and judges. South Carolina Representative Bob Inglis, who introduced the bill to eliminate the centers, adds that "we should not be spending Federal dollars" to pay lawyers "whose sole purpose is to concoct legal theories to frustrate"[23] the death penalty. Other measures to shorten the appeals process, which sometimes takes many years, are being considered by lawmakers at both the state and federal level.

One effect of these measures would be to lower the costs of death penalty cases to the taxpayer. Death penalty supporters claim that life-without-parole sentences put a costly burden on society to feed, clothe, house, supply medical treatment for, and guard murderers. Recently a federally funded Duke University study has come up with figures to show that government costs in death penalty cases are greater than those keeping an offender in prison for life.

South Carolina Representative Bob Inglis introduced a bill that would lower the cost of death penalty cases for taxpayers.

This conclusion has been challenged by pro-capital punishment champions such as New York's State Senator Volker. He points out that the costs did not allow for inflation over the decades a person serving a life sentence might be in prison. According to Senator Volker, many of the trial and appeal costs in life sentence cases are not included in studies by those who want to do away with capital punishment. In any event, he argues, "cost should not be a consideration in deciding whether or not to"[24] execute murderers. As a rule though, those who favor capital punishment believe that money spent caring for lifers would be better spent on more police to protect society from those who kill.

The Pain of Victims' Loved Ones

Some of the survivors of those who have not been protected have a special place among supporters of the death penalty. The issue is not just being on one side or the other of an argument or a debate to them. They have suffered a deep personal loss; a loved one has been taken from them—murdered. To some of them the perpetrator is less than human, an animal, and should be made to suffer as their loved one suffered, as they are suffering, and will go on suffering.

Vernon and Elizabeth Harvey were two of these survivors. Their eighteen-year-old daughter Faith was raped and murdered by two men. One of them, Robert Willie, was sentenced to death for the crime. The Harveys thought he deserved to die. Vernon Harvey told a board considering clemency for Willie that "there is really only one way that we can be absolutely sure that he will never kill again. . . . I would like Mr. Robert Lee Willie's life to end here."[25] Executing Robert Willie gave Vernon and Elizabeth Harvey the opportunity to come to terms with their loss. They watched him die in the electric chair. They were not sorry.

Nine States That Have Resumed Executions Since 1990[26]

State	Last Execution	Resumed Execution
California	1967	April 21, 1992
Delaware	1946	March 14, 1992
Idaho	1957	January 6, 1994
Illinois	1962	September 12, 1990
Maryland	1961	May 17, 1994
Montana	1943	May 10, 1995
Nebraska	1959	September 2, 1994
Pennsylvania	1963	May 2, 1995
Washington	1965	January 5, 1993

4

The Case Against
Executions

People in the cities of eighteenth-century England
usually kept their money in purses with drawstrings. The
purses were knotted to their belts, tied around their
waists, or secured to their person in some other way.
They were tucked into pockets or waistbands. As a rule
the money in the purses was in the form of gold or silver
coins, rather than bills.

In those days, the streets of the cities were very
crowded. People could not help pressing against each
other as they moved through the marketplaces. Among
the crowds were increasing numbers of thieves with nim-
ble fingers and sharp blades who cut the cords attached
to purses and deftly removed them from pockets and
waistbands. These thieves were at first known as cut-
purses, and later called pickpockets.

There was so much of this kind of thievery that
London and other cities passed laws declaring that those

caught stealing in this manner would be put to death. Furthermore, as a lesson to other such thieves, the executions would be performed in public. Crowds gathered to watch the criminals be put to death. There were more pockets picked at these public executions than at any other public gathering.

Those against the death penalty use this example to argue that capital punishment does not stop crime. They back this up with a United Nations study that found "no conclusive evidence" of "the deterrent value of the death penalty."[1] They point out that states such as Texas and Florida, which have put to death the most criminals, have higher violent crime rates than states such as New York, which up until just recently has not had any executions since 1963.

Do Executions Make Life Cheap?

A further argument against capital punishment suggests that rather than preventing violent crime, it is a contributing cause of it. Putting murderers to death sends the message that life is cheap. It has a brutalizing effect on society and can push some unstable people over the edge to commit murder.

There is evidence to support this. In May 1979, John Spenkelink was put to death by the state of Florida. It was the first execution in Florida in fifteen years. For three years before—1976, 1977, and 1978—Florida had the lowest murder rate in the state's recent history. However, during the three years following the killing of Spenkelink—1980, 1981, and 1982—Florida recorded its highest murder rates up to that time. In 1980 alone, the year following the Spenkelink execution, there was a 28 percent increase in killings in Florida.

The state of Georgia resumed executions in 1983. The following year the national murder rate dropped 5 percent, but not in Georgia. In 1984, in Georgia, the murder rate went up 20 percent.

In *Dead Man Walking*, her book about her experiences working with prisoners on death row, Roman Catholic nun Helen Prejean discusses an eight-and-a-half-week period in the fall of 1987, during which the state of Louisiana put to death eight convicted criminals. During the period immediately following, the murder rate in Louisiana's largest and most famous city, New

Sister Helen Prejean wrote the book *Dead Man Walking* about the experiences she had working with death row prisoners.

Orleans, rose 16.39 percent. "Evidence that executions do not deter crime is conclusive," she insists.[2]

One study cited by Amnesty International focused on the monthly murder rates in New York State between 1907 and 1963, when New York stopped applying the death penalty. During that period there had been more executions in New York than in any other state. The study showed that on average in the month following an execution two additional murders were committed.

Some anti-death penalty supporters carry the statistics a step further. They believe that doing away with capital punishment can actually reduce violent crime. They point to Canada, where the murder rate went down steadily over the ten years after the death penalty for murder was ended in 1976.

How Likely are Mistakes?

Numbers aside, it is the nightmare of a possible mistake that drives many of those who oppose the death penalty to do so. If the government wrongly executes one person, that is reason enough in their eyes to do away with capital punishment. "Few errors made by government officials can compare with the horror of executing a person wrongly convicted of a capital crime,"[3] wrote Hugo Adam Bedau and Michael L. Radelet in their book *Miscarriages of Justice in Potentially Capital Cases.*

Are there such errors? The *Stanford Law Review* reports 350 cases of wrongful convictions of capital crimes in the United States in this century. Of these, fifty-five took place in the 1970s and another twenty occurred between 1980 and 1985. Innocent people were put to death under the law in twenty-three cases.

Others who were mistakenly convicted spent long years on death row. For instance, Randall Dale Adams spent twelve years in a Texas state prison fighting against a sentence of death before his innocence was established. He had been convicted mainly on the basis of a story told by the actual killer. The killer had lied to protect himself before his conscience caught up with him and he confessed to having committed the murder himself. In a strikingly similar case in Illinois, Joseph Burrows was released in 1994 after five years on death row when the chief witness against him admitted to the killing for which Burrows had been sentenced to die.

Even more terrible was the case of Shabaka Waglini. He came within thirteen hours of being put to death by the state of Florida. That is how close it was when an appeals court finally accepted new evidence showing that the prosecutor at his original trial had hidden the fact that the murder bullet had not been fired from Mr. Waglini's gun. He had also persuaded the only witness against Waglini to lie at his trial in exchange for a reduced sentence for another crime.

Court-Appointed Lawyers

Prosecutors overeager for convictions are only one of the obstacles the defendant in a death penalty case must overcome according to those against capital punishment. If the accused is poor, he or she must also often rely on a court-appointed lawyer who may lack experience in criminal law, or who because of the small amount the state pays for such services, may not give the case the attention it deserves. The lawyer may not have the time or money to track down defense witnesses, analyze evidence, or hire medical or psychiatric experts.

An example is the murder trial of Robert Wayne Williams in Louisiana. Williams, a black man, was tried by an all-white jury. He was convicted, sentenced to die, and finally put to death in the electric chair in December 1983. His court-appointed lawyer had spent a total of only eight hours preparing his defense.

There is little doubt that poor people are more likely to fall victim to the death penalty than rich people. Philadelphia Judge Lois Forer wrote:

> The legal system is divided into two separate and unequal systems of justice: one for the rich, in which the courts take limitless time to examine, ponder, consider, and deliberate . . . and hear elaborate, endless appeals . . . the other for the poor, in which hasty guilty pleas and brief hearings are the rule and appeals are the exception.[4]

A former warden of California's San Quentin prison told a United States Senate hearing that capital punishment was "a privilege of the poor."[5] And former governor of Florida Leroy Collins pointed out that "who gets executed is still a freakish thing, and depends on wealth, power and many unusual circumstances. Most who are killed are poor and friendless."[6]

Lack of money also keeps poor convicts sentenced to death from hiring qualified lawyers to file appeals. Much has been made by those who favor the death penalty of so-called *frivolous* appeals delaying the carrying out of executions. In fact, while some death penalty cases may drag on—and for good reason—most do not. The late Supreme Court Justice Thurgood Marshall pointed out that "all capital defendants have not spent years filing frivolous claims in federal courts. Many of these defendants have not yet filed any claims when their execution dates are set."[7]

Racial Bias

Those against the death penalty say that it is biased against nonwhites as well as poor people. According to Amnesty International, while African Americans are 12 percent of the population of the United States, they are roughly 48 percent of the nation's death row population. Although this figure has recently fallen to 40.1 percent, in some southern states the numbers are much higher. In Louisiana, 59 percent of death row inmates are black; in Mississippi, 63 percent.

One reason for this may be the bias of prosecutors in seeking the death penalty. There is evidence that they are much more likely to do so in cases where the victim is white and the accused is black. Also blacks who are convicted of killing whites are more often sentenced to death than any other kinds of offenders. Whites are rarely sentenced to death for killing blacks.

This is borne out by a study of four states—Florida, Georgia, Texas, and Ohio—which accounted for 70 percent of all United States death sentences during a five-year period. The study by Amnesty International showed that blacks who killed whites were sentenced to death five to six times more often than whites who killed

51

whites. Among convicted blacks in Florida, those who killed whites were forty times more likely to be sentenced to death than those who killed blacks. And during that period no white person was sentenced to death for killing a black person. Indeed, the Supreme Court itself has recognized that in cases of capital punishment there is "a discrepancy that appears to correlate with race."[8]

Race and poverty are emotional issues for those who believe that the death penalty by its very nature is unfair. However, their opposition also takes an unemotional dollars-and-cents approach to the question. They point out that the appeals process for those facing the death penalty is costly and time-consuming—not just to the convicted criminal, but to the state and federal government as well.

Alternative Sentencing

According to a study by the New York State Defenders' Association, the average death penalty case—the trial, plus the first stage of appeals following it—costs the government $1.8 million. This is three times as much as it would cost to keep the offender in prison for life. Capital punishment, according to Democratic Senator Ted Kennedy of Massachusetts, "places incredible strain on our criminal justice system." It is "a transparent excuse," he adds, "for inaction on other steps to combat crime."[9]

Death penalty opponents such as Kennedy and former New York governor Mario Cuomo do not wish to be thought soft on crime. Kennedy has consistently backed strong anti-crime legislation in the Senate, while Cuomo as governor spoke out for life sentences without parole as an alternative to capital punishment. Many who are against the death penalty favor replacing it with strong anti-crime measures and harsh sentencing.

They are particularly sympathetic to the families of murder victims. Activist nun Helen Prejean has gone out of her way to contact, befriend, and help the families of murder victims—even those who do not agree with her anti-capital punishment stand. But Sister Helen, along with most of those against the death penalty, believes that statements by those whose loved ones have been killed should not be heard in court, where they influence the sentencing of offenders convicted of murder. The emotions raised are simply too powerful not to affect the sentencing process.

However, not all relatives who survive murder victims are for capital punishment. Roy Persons of St. Petersburg, Florida, whose wife was killed, came out against the sentence of death for her murderer. He believed that it would only "reinforce and perpetuate feelings of vengeance, hate and further human evil."[10]

Jury Selection

Should someone who has views like those of Roy Persons not be allowed to serve on juries where a sentence of death might follow conviction? Prosecutors routinely find ways to exclude those who hold such views from jury service in these cases. This is not fair, say those opposed to capital punishment. It loads the dice in favor of the prosecution and encourages the handing down of death sentences. Why, they ask, should one who

Not all families of murder victims are for the death penalty. Camille Bell, whose child was murdered in Atlanta, spoke out against capital punishment at a rally in 1990.

approves the death penalty be considered any more fair-minded a juror than one who opposes it?

Far more disturbing than such questions to them is the act of execution itself. The Constitution of the United States, they point out, forbids "cruel and unusual punishments."[11] But every means of execution, past and present, involves suffering, and often that suffering can be extreme. By definition, those opposed to capital punishment insist that putting someone to death who would not otherwise die is cruel and unusual punishment.

Furthermore the act turns the executioners—the attendants who administer the fatal drug, the guard who breaks the cyanide gas capsule, the shooter on the firing squad, those who pull the switch—into murderers. True, these people are only doing their job, only acting for the state. But, opponents to capital punishment say, execution corrupts the government itself. It breeds disrespect for law. It brutalizes society.

Executions create a climate that holds life cheap. They do exactly the opposite of what they are meant to do. They encourage, rather than deter, murder. Capital punishment denies the sanctity of human life. Society says that killing is wrong, but then it kills the killer. If it is wrong for a murderer to take a life, how can it be right for the state to take a life?

5

The Law and How it Changes

Like other state laws, capital punishment laws are different in each of the fifty states of the United States. The differences are not just between states that ban the death penalty and those that allow it, but also among those that enforce it according to laws that may vary greatly. These variations have to do with which crimes deserve capital punishment, which persons may and may not be executed, the method by which those condemned may be put to death, and various other issues. However, all state laws applying to the death penalty must agree with federal law as defined by the United States Supreme Court.

The Supreme Court bases its judgments on the Constitution of the United States, the amendments to it, various laws passed by Congress, executive orders issued by the president, and a collection of past English and American laws. This collection determines what are called precedents—decisions that courts have recognized as legal in the past. Precedents, along with the Constitution, are the most important elements the justices of the Supreme Court consider when determining questions of law.

These justices are part of an ever-changing group. Justices retire or die, and new ones take their place. They are chosen by the president and approved by the Senate, and so politics plays a large role in their joining the Supreme Court. One Court may not agree with another, and so we say we have liberal Courts or conservative Courts or middle-of-the-road Courts. Also the individual justices on a Court may disagree with how the law should be understood. There are nine justices on the Court, and the votes are sometimes as close as five-to-four. This is particularly true with such emotional and explosive issues as the death penalty.

Consider the 1947 case of Willie Francis. He had been sentenced to die in the electric chair in Louisiana. However, when the sentence was carried out, there was a mechanical failure and Willie did not die. He appealed to the Supreme Court to stop his being executed a second time. He said that would be a cruel and unusual punishment forbidden by the Constitution. The court denied his appeal by the narrow vote of five-to-four.

Justice Stanley F. Reed spoke for the majority. "The fact that petitioner has already been subjected to a current of electricity," he said, "does not make his subsequent execution any more cruel in the constitutional sense than any other execution."[1] Justices William O. Douglas,

Harold H. Burton, Frank Murphy, and Wiley B. Rutledge disagreed with the decision.

The judgment against Willie Frances only carried a short step further the traditional Supreme Court view that the "cruel and unusual punishments"[2] clause in the Eighth Amendment to the Constitution does not apply to the death penalty. This had been confirmed by the Court in case after case during the nineteenth and early twentieth centuries. Furthermore majority public opinion during this time had almost always supported the death penalty.

Public Opinion

Supreme Court justices are not supposed to be influenced by public opinion, but they are only human. In 1947, the year Willie Francis was put to death, there were 152 executions in the United States. That number dropped to seven by 1965, and in 1967, there was only one execution in the entire country. By that time, according to *The Encyclopedia of American Crime*, "public opinion was overwhelmingly opposed to the death penalty."[3]

The time was ripe for a group of organizations against capital punishment to confront Florida and California, the states with the largest death row populations. Actions to outlaw the death penalty were based on several constitutional points. The issues raised were so complicated that not only Florida and California, but all other states stopped executing offenders while they were considered. No convicted criminals were put to death in the United States during the next ten years.

Now considered cruel and unusual punishment, crowds once gathered to witness the public whipping of criminals.

In 1968, when the Court heard the case of *Witherspoon* v. *Illinois*, the justices could not help but be aware of the shift in public opinion against capital punishment. What was surprising was that they mentioned that shift in the judgment they handed down. It was the first sign that the Court would be swayed by majority attitudes towards the death penalty over the next two decades.

Witherspoon v. *Illinois* raised the question of whether people opposed to the death penalty could be legally excluded from juries in cases where capital punishment might play a part. Should this view alone be cause for their being dismissed from the panels from which death penalty juries are selected? The Court decided that it could not.

Justice Potter Stewart spoke for the majority:

> In a nation less than half of whose people believe in the death penalty, a jury composed exclusively of such people [those favoring capital punishment] cannot speak for the community. . . . Such a jury can speak only for a distinct and dwindling minority. . . . In its quest for a jury capable of imposing the death penalty, the State produced a jury uncommonly willing to condemn a man to die.[4]

Sentencing by Jury

Three years after *Witherspoon* v. *Illinois*, the Court was asked to decide if state laws that left it to juries alone to decide on death sentences violated the Constitution. The point raised was that while juries could decide guilt or innocence, they should not decide on punishment; that was for judges to do. The case was *McGautha* v. *California*. By a six-to-three vote, the Court found that giving "the jury the power to pronounce life or death in capital cases" was not "offensive to anything in the Constitution."[5]

The following year, on June 29, 1972, the Supreme Court handed down a decision in the case of *Furman* v. *Georgia* that "effectively reversed *McGautha*" and "invalidated all existing death penalty statutes."[6] The vote was five-to-four. At first it seemed a major victory for opponents of capital punishment. The death penalty appeared to be no longer legal in the United States.

Key to the meaning of the decision, however, was its very careful wording: "As the statutes are administered . . . the imposition and carrying out of the death penalty [constitutes] cruel and unusual punishment in violation of Eighth and Fourteenth Amendments."[7]

Although the decision was widely understood by the general public to have outlawed the death penalty, that is not what it did. It only said that it was illegal as it was now *administered* by the various states. It left open the possibility of restoring the death penalty if it was handled differently.

Over the next four years, as public opinion once again shifted, this time in favor of capital punishment, thirty-five states revised their death penalty laws in ways that they thought would satisfy the Supreme Court. Their efforts came to a head in the case of *Gregg* v. *Georgia*. The Court began hearing it on March 30, 1976. The scene has been described as follows:

61

Lawyers, reporters, and spectators crowd the courtroom. For two days, the justices will hear arguments by ten lawyers in cases from five different states. The lives of six men are at stake in these arguments. Each was convicted of murder and sentenced to die. And each has challenged the state law under which the sentence was imposed.[8]

"Society's Moral Outrage"

Although the cases were grouped together, the Court focused on *Gregg* v. *Georgia*. If Georgia's revised death penalty statutes were legal, they would set certain standards for other states.

Troy Gregg had been convicted of armed robbery and murder. He and another hitchhiker had robbed and killed two men who picked them up, and had then stolen the car. When they were caught by police in the stolen car, a .25 caliber pistol was found in Gregg's pocket. It was later determined that the pistol had fired the bullets that killed the two murdered men. Faced with this evidence, Gregg signed a confession.

A jury found Gregg guilty. Under the revised Georgia laws, the jury then considered his sentence. The jurors found that the motive of the murder was to steal money. They also found that he had committed the murder in connection with two other crimes—the armed robbery of each of the two victims. These conditions satisfied the new law, and so the jurors sentenced Gregg to death. But did the laws under which Gregg was sentenced satisfy the Supreme Court's objections in *Furman* v. *Georgia*?

By a vote of seven-to-two, the Court decided that the

revised Georgia law "under which Gregg was sentenced to death does not violate the Constitution."[9] Justice Potter Stewart spoke of recent public opinion polls showing heavy public support for capital punishment. He said this made the death penalty a legitimate "expression of society's moral outrage"[10] towards murder.

The decisions the Court handed down on July 2, 1976, upheld some new state laws, but not others. The Court devoted over two hundred pages to the five cases. It approved laws that spelled out jury guidelines, but not those that called for death sentences without regard to circumstances.

As to the six condemned offenders in the five cases that had been decided, the death sentences for three were struck down. The sentences for the other three were allowed to stand. Troy Gregg's sentence was upheld.

Who Should Die?

The year after *Gregg* v. *Georgia* restored the death penalty, the Supreme Court took up the question of the crimes to which it should be applied. There was general agreement as to first-degree murder and treason, but what about such crimes as rape and kidnapping? On June 20, 1977, the court decided in *Everheart* v. *Georgia* and *Coker* v. *Georgia* that neither crime could be punished by death. By a majority of five-to-four, the Court decided that the death penalty "is an excessive penalty for the rapist" because "the murderer kills; the rapist . . . does not."[11] The same logic was applied to kidnappers who did not kill their victims.

That year, 1977, Gary Gilmore was executed by

firing squad. Other executions in other states followed slowly, then more and more quickly. Among those executed were juvenile offenders—those convicted of committing murder before they reached the age of eighteen.

James Terry Roach was one of these juvenile offenders. In October 1977, he was seventeen years old with a history of juvenile crime already behind him. He had served time in a reform school from which he had escaped. Now, armed with a gun, he fell in with a boy his own age and an older man who supplied the youths with alcohol and drugs.

All three were high while driving down a South Carolina back road when they came upon a parked car with people in it. Roach pulled out his gun and shot the man behind the wheel three times in the head. Then he pulled the man's fourteen-year-old daughter out of the car and he and his two companions raped her. She, too, was killed.

When the two boys and the man were arrested and convicted of the crime, there was a public outcry for the death penalty. There was, however, evidence that Roach had been under the influence of the older man as well as the alcohol that he had drunk and the drugs that he had taken. And he may have been in the early stages of a brain ailment called Huntington's disease at the time he committed the crime.

The jury did not accept these factors as an excuse for his crime. They felt that his total disregard for human life more than outweighed any mitigating circumstances.

They found overwhelming legal justification for a sentence of death and imposed it.

Although the general public approved the sentence, there were appeals for mercy. Among those who asked South Carolina Governor Richard W. Riley to spare Roach were United Nations Secretary General Javier Perez de Cuellar, former United States President Jimmy Carter, and Nobel Prize winning humanitarian Mother Teresa. But the governor refused.

The execution was delayed four times while appeals were heard and denied. A final appeal to the United States Supreme Court was also denied. On January 10, 1986, James Terry Roach was strapped into the electric chair. His last words, which he had a hard time reading, were roughly these: "I pray that my fate will someday save another kid from the wrong side of the tracks."[12] His difficulty reading the statement may have been due to terror or remorse or simply to his lack of reading skills.

Meanwhile, as described by Elaine Landau in her book *Teens and the Death Penalty*, "a crowd gathered outside the prison compound. They had come to cheer the execution of an individual with a mental age of twelve for a crime he'd committed when he was seventeen."[13]

Should Minors Be Executed?

Two years later, the United States Supreme Court considered the question of executing minors. The case was *Thompson* v. *Oklahoma*. The Court ruled that minors could indeed be put to death.

Opponents of capital punishment were outraged. The Court had been ambiguous about a cut-off age for

65

James Terry Roach, while intoxicated and high, murdered a man and then raped and murdered his fourteen-year-old daughter. He was executed for his crimes.

executing youthful offenders. Many state laws had not set one. Among those that did, Indiana drew the line at ten-year-olds; Montana, at twelve-year-olds; and Mississippi, at thirteen-year-olds. The death penalty opponents pointed out that both the Court and the states were in violation of the 1966 United Nations *International Covenant on Civil and Political Rights,* which says that "sentence of death shall not be imposed for crimes committed by persons below eighteen years of age."[14]

Five months after Roach was executed, on June 24, 1986, there was another execution in the state of Georgia. This one focused public attention on another capital punishment question that the Supreme Court would have to decide: Was it legal to execute offenders who were mentally retarded?

The executed man was Jerome Bowden, a thirty-three-year-old African-American man with an IQ of 65—at least 35 points below the normal IQ range of 100–120. He had been convicted of the murder of Kathryn Stryker on the basis of his own confession. The confession had been typed by the police, and Bowden—who could neither read nor write—had signed it by making his mark. The prosecutor had excluded all African Americans from the jury that tried him. The trial judge had denied Bowden's lawyer's request that a psychiatrist test Bowden's mental competence to stand trial. One of his appeal lawyers called his death sentence "a meaningless act of vengeance."[15] Nevertheless, it was carried out.

In 1989, the Supreme Court ruled that executions of low-IQ offenders such as Bowden were permitted under law. The case was *Penry* v. *Lynaugh*. In deciding it, the Court said that the Eighth Amendment did not prohibit the execution of the mentally retarded.

Tightening the Noose

Since then, the trend at both the federal and state level has been towards stricter enforcement of the death penalty. At the same time, there has also been a trend by states and the federal government to exclude those who are mentally retarded from the death penalty. Sections of crime bills being considered in 1995 seek to shorten the expensive and lengthy appeals process in capital punishment cases. Many prosecutors agree with South Carolina's Attorney General Charlie Condon, who believes that the appeal lawyers' real "goal is to stop executions at any cost."[16] In reply, Gerald H. Goldstein, president of the National Association of Criminal Defense Lawyers, points out that "a high body count without a fair legal process is simply wrong."[17]

A federal law that states that the government must provide lawyers for offenders sentenced to death is still in effect. A provision of a 1995 bill passed by Congress would have eliminated funding for death penalty resource centers to file petitions on behalf of prisoners in the federal courts, but the president has refused to sign the bill into law. According to *The New York Times*, it would have insured that "the nearly 3,000 inmates awaiting execution" will no longer be served by "the 190 lawyers nationwide paid with Federal dollars to represent them"[18] in the federal courts.

But what about the already existing law, which as Chief Judge Richard Arnold of the United States Court of Appeals for the Eighth Circuit points out, requires the government to "appoint and pay for counsel in death-penalty cases"?[19] There is a conflict. Just what constitutes *adequate* counsel in capital cases just might be the next death penalty question the Supreme Court will have to decide.

6

Where to Live and Where to Die

Geography often decides whether a person convicted of a capital crime in the United States will live or die. The state in which the offender is tried, the city, even the county or township, are life-and-death matters to the defendant. They can influence every stage of the proceedings from arrest to sentencing. Location determines if the crime is punishable by death, whether the prosecutor will seek the death penalty, how able the defense is, who will decide the punishment when the verdict is guilty, how the appeals process will be treated by state courts, how sympathetic a federal appeals court may be at the lower levels, the chances of appeals for clemency, and the procedures for last-minute pardons on death row. The differences among locations in how a case is handled can be as wide as that between states with a death penalty and those without one. It is local policy, frequently at the lowest level, that can put a case on the death penalty track.

The first people who make decisions affecting whether or not a crime is a death penalty case are the arresting officers. Their report will be the initial contact with the case by the prosecutor's office. Typically an assistant district attorney will study the police paperwork on the crime. This will include the arrest report—detailing the circumstances of the crime insofar as they are known and the arrest—interrogation reports of the suspect by the police, and any statements that the accused may have made. After reading this material, the assistant district attorney will recommend whether or not to seek the death penalty.

Rule 352

In most states this will mean filling out some sort of death penalty form. In Pennsylvania this form is called a "*Notice of Aggravating Circumstances.*"[1] It is commonly called a "352"—after Rule 352 passed by the Pennsylvania legislature in 1989.

Rule 352 states that the prosecutor must inform the defense attorney within ten days after the accused prisoner's first appearance in court that the death penalty is a possibility and state the reason or reasons why it is. The 352 form lists sixteen possible reasons, among them that the murder was committed during the commission of another crime, that it was planned and executed in a cold-blooded way, that the victim was a child under the age of twelve, or a police officer, or a witness in a trial who had not yet been heard. These reasons are called

States With Capital Punishment Laws (38)[2]
(As of May 1995)

Alabama	Kentucky	Ohio
Arizona	Louisiana	Oklahoma
Arkansas	Maryland	Oregon
California	Mississippi	Pennsylvania
Colorado	Missouri	South Carolina
Connecticut	Montana	South Dakota
Delaware	Nebraska	Tennessee
Florida	Nevada	Texas
Georgia	New Hampshire	Utah
Idaho	New Jersey	Virginia
Illinois	New Mexico	Washington
Indiana	New York	Wyoming
Kansas	North Carolina	

"aggravators,"[3] and in Pennsylvania they make the difference between an ordinary murder trial and a trial in which the penalty may be death.

The assistant district attorney who fills out a 352 form is, of course, responsible to his or her boss, the district attorney. The final decision as to whether or not to go for the death penalty will be up to the district attorney. He or she is the first one to officially make this life-and-death decision.

District attorneys build their reputations on successful prosecutions. Crime is a major concern in most cities and counties of the United States, and political careers can be made or broken on the issue of the death penalty. People on both sides of the capital punishment issue agree that death penalty cases are decided at a local level.[4]

Philadelphia, where Pennsylvania senator and 1996 Republican presidential candidate Arlen Specter made his early reputation as a district attorney who strongly supported capital punishment, is a good example. Pennsylvania is the only northeastern state to put a person to death since 1967. Philadelphia is the city in the Northeast where an offender is most likely to face the death penalty. Of those on Pennsylvania's death row, 55 percent are from Philadelphia. Much of the responsibility—or credit, depending which side of the death penalty issue one is on—must go to fifty-four-year-old Philadelphia District Attorney Lynne Abraham.

"When it comes to the death penalty, I am passionate."[5] says Ms. Abraham. "I've looked at all those sentenced to be executed," she insists. "No one will shed a tear. Prison is too good for them. They don't deserve to

Number of Inmates on Death Row by State[6]
(Total of 2,943 as of December 31, 1994)

California	396	Louisiana	41
Texas	390	Arkansas	38
Florida	349	Kentucky	28
Pennsylvania	168	Idaho	21
Illinois	163	Delaware	14
North Carolina	145	Maryland	14
Ohio	137	Oregon	14
Alabama	131	Washington	13
Oklahoma	124	Utah	11
Arizona	122	Nebraska	9
Georgia	105	New Jersey	9
Tennessee	101	Montana	8
Missouri	92	Connecticut	5
Nevada	70	Colorado	3
South Carolina	57	New Mexico	2
Virginia	55	South Dakota	2
Indiana	53	Federal Law	6
Mississippi	53	Military Law	8

(Note: Death penalty states not mentioned had no inmates on death row at time of survey.)

live. I represent the victim and the family. I don't care about killers."[7] District Attorney Abraham is very popular. Support for capital punishment in Philadelphia, as in the rest of the country, runs from 75 percent to 80 percent.

However, the district attorney of Pittsburgh's Allegheny County, Robert E. Colville, is equally popular although he does not share Abraham's passion for capital punishment. "I never had a lot of thought that the ultimate revenge was necessary," says Colville. "The death penalty can't cure everything."[8] In 1994, Philadelphia asked for the death penalty in 159 cases, about 39 percent of the 404 murders brought to trial. Pittsburgh sought it in eight cases, less than 8 percent of the 104 murders prosecuted.

Philadelphia also had a pro-death penalty judge in Albert F. Sabo, now retired. Judge Sabo sentenced thirty-two offenders to death, more than any other judge in the country.

The bottom line is that a Pennsylvania murderer tried in Philadelphia stands a far greater chance of being sentenced to death than one who stands trial in Pittsburgh. This does not, however, mean that a Philadelphian sentenced to death—or any Pennsylvanian on death row for that matter—is likely to die. Of the 190 men and four women on Pennsylvania's death row—the fourth largest death row of any state in the country— only two have been executed. Indeed Pennsylvania offers more hope to condemned offenders than states with much smaller death row populations, but much higher execution rates. Louisiana, for instance, had forty-one prisoners on death row as of the end of 1994, but had already executed twenty-one offenders since capital punishment was restored by the Supreme Court.

The state in which a prisoner is sentenced to death can be as important to his or her chances of survival as the death sentence itself. California death rows led the country with 396 inmates as of the end of 1994, but California has only executed two people. Texas, on the other hand, with 390 death row inmates, up to that time had carried out executions of eighty-five offenders— fourteen in 1994 alone. Illinois had sentenced 163 people to death, but only executed 2, while Arkansas sentenced only 38, but executed 9.

Pennsylvania is not the only state where different cities take widely different approaches to the death penalty. In New York State, where the death penalty had just been restored, there is a marked contrast in the way upstate and downstate district attorneys regard it. It has long been taken for granted that the first death penalty case under the new law would be prosecuted upstate, where both the people and the prosecutors most strongly favor it.

D. A.s Disagree

A case deserving of prosecutors' enthusiasm shook the small city of Kingston in late September 1995. A seven-year-old girl named Rickel Knox was kidnapped and murdered, allegedly by a twenty-five-year-old friend of her family named Lawrence Whitehurst. She may or may not have been raped.

Kingston is in upstate Ulster County in New York.

The district attorney of Ulster County is E. Michael Kavanaugh, a strong supporter of the death penalty. Following a statement by Whitehurst, which led to the discovery of the little girl's body, District Attorney Kavanaugh announced that he would ask for the death penalty in this case. There was wide approval of this decision among the twenty-three thousand residents of Kingston.

When the case comes to trial though, there may be a hitch. In order to find the child, Kavanaugh agreed to sign a plea bargain deal with Whitehurst—an agreement not to seek the death penalty. When Rickel Knox was found dead, the district attorney announced that he would not honor the deal. "I would have done a deal with the devil to get that child back safely to her parents," he told reporters. "It is not an enforceable agreement."[9]

Only time will tell whether it is or not, but prosecutors less eager to bring a death penalty case might balk at such a tactic. It is unlikely that it would have been used by at least two of downstate New York City's five district attorneys. One of the two, Robert Morgenthau, has written and argued against capital punishment on the grounds that rather than helping the fight against crime, it hurts it. Juries, he believes, are more reluctant to convict when the penalty is so final. Since the death penalty became law, Morgenthau has vowed that "I intend to exercise that discretion wisely."[10]

District Attorney Robert T. Johnson of New York City's Bronx County goes even further in his opposition to capital punishment than Morgenthau. He has said

Number of Executions by State Since 1976[11]
(Total of 300 as of October 5, 1995)

State	Total Executions	1994 Executions	1995 Executions Through Oct. 5
Texas	100	14	14
Florida	34	1	1
Virginia	27	2	3
Louisiana	22	0	1
Georgia	20	1	2
Missouri	14	0	3
Alabama	12	0	2
Arkansas	11	5	2
North Carolina	7	1	1
Nevada	5	0	0
Delaware	5	1	1
Mississippi	4	0	0
South Carolina	5	0	1
Utah	4	0	0
Arizona	4	0	0
Indiana	3	1	0
Oklahoma	6	0	3
California	2	0	0
Illinois	6	1	3
Pennsylvania	2	0	2
Washington	2	1	0
Idaho	1	1	0
Maryland	1	1	0
Montana	1	0	1
Nebraska	1	1	0
Wyoming	1	0	0
Totals	300	31	40

that he will never seek the death penalty because of his "intense respect for the value and sanctity of human life."[12] When New York Governor Pataki protested that "the people have spoken loudly and clearly through the democratic process that they want the death penalty"[13] and suggested that Johnson should step aside so that someone else might prosecute death penalty cases, Johnson pointed out that "the law is that district attorneys have the discretion."[14]

That is, of course, the point. It is one reason why there are such wide variations in death penalty prosecutions among districts and cities in states. Another reason has to do with regional attitudes—city and country, small town and suburb, Northeast and South and Midwest and West.

Between 1976 and the beginning of October 1995, the overwhelming number of executions in the United States took place in the South. Almost five times as many death sentences (248) were carried out in the South than in any other region of the country. By contrast, there were twenty-one executions in the West, twenty-nine in the Midwest and only two in the Northeast. The charts in this chapter tell not only where the death penalty is legal, but also where it is most often handed down, and where it is most often actually carried out.

The Lengthy Appeals Process

Use of the death penalty mounted in the first ten months of 1995. As of October 5, there were nine more executions carried out in the United States than in all of 1994. Pennsylvania's first execution in thirty-three years

George Pataki was elected governor of New York partly for his pro-death penalty stance.

took place on May 2, 1995. Since the death penalty was restored in 1976, the number of executions had risen from a low of one in 1977 to a high of thirty-eight in 1993—two less than in 1995 with three months still to go.

During this time some appeals have kept sentenced offenders awaiting execution on death row for as long as twenty-one years. However, experts on both sides of the capital punishment question agree that if pending federal legislation to shorten the appeals process succeeds, such delays will be greatly shortened and the number of executions each year will grow. Is this justified because it shortens the torture of waiting by the condemned as those favoring such legislation say? Or will it, as opponents claim, simply add to a body count that serves no purpose save revenge?

Who Should be Executed, and Who Should Not?

When he murdered three elderly people in Georgia, John Young was not insane. At eighteen years old he was not under age. He was not defending himself. He did not kill in self-defense; he did not kill by accident. He was not under the influence of another person. There was no doubt he was guilty of the crime of murder.

But John Young had taken a lot of drugs just before the murder, and they had blurred his judgment. Also, John Young had a particularly terrible childhood. When he was only three years old, he had watched his mother being murdered in bed as he lay beside her. He had been raised by an alcoholic relative who abused him. He had been thrown out of the house at an early age and forced by circumstance to support himself as a child prostitute. He learned to use drugs as a way of getting through the long, unpleasant nights.

The jury that tried John Young for murder heard

nothing of this. John Young's court-appointed lawyer did not investigate John's background. He later admitted that he had spent "hardly any time preparing for the case."[1] Shortly after John's trial, the lawyer was disbarred and forbidden to practice law any more.

John Young was convicted and sentenced to death. While he waited for the sentence to be carried out, various appeals to have it set aside were filed. The appeals pointed out that because of the drugs he had taken, John had not been in his right mind at the time of the murders. They introduced a statement by his lawyer detailing his lack of attention to the case. They presented John Young's childhood history and pointed out that had the judge and jury been told of it, although John Young would surely have been found guilty, he might not have been sentenced to death.

The United States district court and the court of appeals were not swayed. They refused to set aside the death penalty verdict. John Young was executed.

What Excuses Murder?

But the questions raised by his case have not gone away. If a person commits a crime while under the influence of alcohol or drugs, should that be a reason to punish the offender less severely? Modern medicine regards alcoholism as a disease. To some extent drug addiction is also looked at that way. If a person is sick, and the sickness is partly responsible for the crime he or she commits, should society not be understanding? Even if the crime is murder, shouldn't the penalty be less harsh?

And what about a childhood like John Young's?

Shouldn't that count? Didn't it teach him to be brutal? Didn't he watch his mother being murdered? Didn't he grow up with violence? Wasn't that all he knew? Children do what they see done; they do what is done to them; and when they become adults, they are only grown up children. How can we blame John Young for what he was allowed to become by the world in which he grew up? How can we execute him?

"Whoa!" supporters of capital punishment protest. John Young killed three defenseless old people in cold blood. Lots of people who had miserable childhoods never did anything like that. The world is not fair, and some kids get better breaks than other kids, but that does not mean we can let the other kids grow up and get away with murder.

So what if John Young was under the influence of drugs? According to New Yorkers Against the Death Penalty, "two-thirds of homicides in this country involve alcohol or drugs."[2] Does that mean those murderers should not be punished?

And as for his lawyer, the court ruled that he had been legally competent to handle this case. The court decided that Young's past did not excuse him. He may have had bad breaks, but not as bad as the break his three victims got when he got high and killed them. Did John Young deserve to die? You bet he did!

The argument is about what are called mitigating circumstances. These are factors that may not relate directly to the crime of murder itself, but that are sometimes used to establish the degree of guilt of the one accused of committing it. Guilt is not always an absolute. The law recognizes this. That is why less than 3 percent of the murders committed in the United States every year are punished by sentences of death.

The O. J. Question

California has capital punishment, but in the murder trial of football star O. J. Simpson, a case in which the victims—his ex-wife and a male friend—had their throats brutally slashed, the state did not seek the death penalty. Instead, Simpson was charged with first-degree murder, for which the punishment was life in prison without parole, and second-degree murder, which carried a sentence of twenty-five years to life and meant that with good behavior he could go free in seven years. As it turned out, Simpson was found not guilty of all charges.

But the question remains: Why did the prosecution not ask for the death penalty in the Simpson case? On what basis does the state decide to bring a death penalty charge? How do the 3 percent of murder cases where it is asked for differ from the 97 percent where it is not? Is it fair that those who prosecute decide in advance what are and what are not mitigating circumstances? Do those who deserve it escape the death penalty? Are those deserving of mercy executed? What are the guidelines that decide who should be executed and who should not?

The first guideline is the nature of the crime. In most death penalty states that means the crime of murder, sometimes other crimes, sometimes not. But what sort of murder, and of who, and under what circumstances?

For instance, it is late at night and a driver is traveling sixty-five miles an hour on a highway where the speed limit is fifty-five. A young man in dark clothing darts across the highway. The driver hits the brake, but it is too late. The young man is struck by the car and killed. The driver is charged with vehicular homicide—murder with an automobile or truck.

The charge, however, does not carry a death sentence. By driving above the speed limit, the driver was not careful of human life as the law requires, and so is responsible for the death. But it was never the driver's *intent* to kill. *Intent* is most important in separating death penalty cases from ordinary murder cases—even when they are not this clear-cut.

Even if the driver had been drunk, lack of intent would have kept prosecutors from seeking the death penalty. However, lack of intent is not always reason enough to save the offender from capital punishment. The circumstances of a murder also count.

Say an unarmed man snatches a woman's purse and runs away. A police officer sees the crime, pulls out his gun and gives chase. The officer catches the purse-snatcher, and there is a scuffle during which the officer's gun goes off, killing the officer. The purse snatcher is now subject to the death penalty in most of those states that have one.

The New York State death penalty law, similar to other laws in death penalty states around the country, insures that if "the victim was killed while the defendant was in the course of committing, attempting to commit, or in the course of immediate flight after committing"[3] a crime, the death penalty may be sought. Most death penalty states, like New York, also provide for its use when the "victim was a police officer . . . engaged in the course of performing his official duties."[4]

Capital punishment supporters strongly believe that it should be used in cases where the victim is an officer of the law. Some opponents of the death penalty—not all—ask why the life of a police officer, who is paid to put himself or herself at risk, should be considered more valuable than the life of an ordinary citizen. Supporters answer that the rule of law is the very foundation of our society and the slaying of a law officer is a direct assault upon it.

In many death penalty states, their point of view extends to include murders of all peace officers, judges, witnesses to crimes and their families, and prison personnel. These murders are viewed as attacks on the law itself. In other words, the killing not only deprives a person or persons of life, but also does great harm by undermining the legal system.

Death for Terrorists

Following the 1995 bombing of the Federal Building in Oklahoma City, in which at least 167 people, including 15 children, were killed,[5] there was a public outcry for terrorists to be executed. The bill would have made capital crimes committed on federal property or against federal agents subject to the death penalty. It also would have limited most state and federal "death-row prisoners to one appeal in Federal court."[6]

President Bill Clinton supported the bill. It "passed the Senate by the lopsided vote of 91 to 8" and "a similar measure was approved by the House Judiciary

Committee by a vote of 23 to 12."[7] However, the full House has not passed the bill and opposition to it is mounting. "There's a growing feeling that the legislation goes way too far,"[8] says Representative Bob Barr, a Georgia Republican and former United States attorney.

Even before the Oklahoma City bombing, a growing number of incidents had aroused support for capital punishment for terrorists. Professor Robert A. Friedlander who teaches law at Ohio Northern University recommended "the death penalty for terrorists who cause loss of life in any fashion" and called for the "sentence to be carried out via public execution."[9] He believed that "carrying out that sentence via public execution, without an inordinate delay, may do wonders for restoring public order to a global community."[10]

Amnesty International disagrees, pointing to evidence that "executions are as likely to increase acts of terror as to stop them."[11] Manachem Begin, who, before he served as prime minister of Israel, led a group of freedom fighters seeking independence from British rule, said that when the death penalty was applied to his comrades, it only "made us more efficient and dedicated to the cause."[12] He added that the British "were not sentencing our terrorists to death" but rather their "own people, and we decided how many."[13]

Executing Drug Dealers

Another effort to extend federal use of capital punishment is the Drug Kingpin Death Penalty Act sponsored by New York Senator Alphonse D'Amato. Pointing to over one million drug arrests annually,

DEAD!

Story on page 3

RUTH BROWN SNYDER   **HENRY JUDD GRAY**

SING SING'S DEATH CHAIR COLLECTS TWOFOLD FOR ALBERT SNYDER'S MURDER!—Sex attraction—illicit love—and finally murder: For those things last night the state shocked out the lives of Ruth Snyder and Judd Gray in the electric chair. Ruth was pronounced dead at 11:06; Judd at 11:14. "Father, forgive them, they don't know what they're doing," were last words of Ruth, condemned convict No. CC79892. Gray, condemned convict No. CC79891, mumbled a prayer.

—Story on page 3, also a picture, page 21 and back pa

In a famous scandal, Ruth Brown Snyder and Henry Judd Gray murdered Snyder's husband after she took out a $48,000 life insurance policy on him. The lovers were given the death penalty for their crime in 1928.

D'Amato suggests cutting drugs off at the source with death sentences for major drug dealers. His bill would also apply to anyone who "engages in a Federal drug felony, and a person dies in the course of the offense or from the use of drugs involved in the offense."[14] William Bennett, the "Drug Czar" in charge of fighting the war against drugs under President Bush, went even further, urging the death penalty for "the high-level banker"[15] who launders money for the drug trade.

Even before Senator D'Amato introduced his bill, there was opposition to the idea of a death penalty for drug dealers. Writing in *The New York Times* on September 16, 1988, Franklin E. Zimring called the idea "not only barbaric but also foolish."[16] He added that "it holds no promise for suppressing the drug trade, and may even be counterproductive."[17]

Military Justice

The death penalty is already authorized by the United States government under the Federal Air Piracy Act of 1974, which limits its use to crimes of "aircraft piracy resulting in death."[18] It is also legal under the armed forces' "Uniform Code of Military Justice (UCMJ)" which lists a dozen crimes—felony murder, espionage, and desertion among them—as punishable by death when committed in time of war."[19] However, only one member of the military has been executed for desertion since the Civil War—Private Edward Donald Slovick, executed in 1945 by a firing squad of fellow World War II soldiers obeying an order signed by General Dwight D. Eisenhower.

Some people thought back then, and think now, that Private Slovick should not have been executed. He was afraid to die, so he ran away. He was caught—and he was killed. Others believe that when so many others were fighting—and dying—it was simple justice to shoot a coward who ran out on his fellow soldiers.

The arguments surrounding capital punishment are different today, but the feelings run just as high; and there are still more questions than answers. Should assassinations of government officials be punishable by death? Should juveniles and mentally retarded people who murder be executed? Should torturers be spared? Serial killers? Mass murderers? Should those who murder out of jealousy, or passion, be treated differently than contract killers who slay for money? There are always more questions to consider, and the answers always come around to this: Who should die? Who should live? Who should decide?

8

Instruments of
Execution

Not long after New York became the thirty-eighth state
to pass a death penalty bill, the State Department of
Correctional Services released a set of procedures for
executions as follows:

Fourteen witnesses are allowed in the execution
chamber.

Eight security officers strap the inmate to a gurney
and wheel him into the execution chamber.

There are two execution technicians. The one in the
chamber attaches intravenous tubes to the
condemned.

The other—known as "the executioner"—remains in
another room where the lethal chemicals will be
injected into tubes that go through the wall into
the execution chamber.

A cardiac monitor is attached to the inmate.

A curtain is opened, allowing the witnesses to view the inmate.

Sodium pentothal is injected to knock the inmate unconscious.

Pavulon is injected to stop his breathing and paralyze his muscles.

Finally, potassium chloride is injected to stop his heart.

The executioner then observes the inmate for five minutes.

A physician examines the inmate and pronounces him dead.[1]

This is the method of execution known as lethal injection, and while the procedures vary from state to state, it is fairly typical. "We didn't see a reason why the public shouldn't know, step by step, the process used for executions," said James B. Flateau, the Corrections Department spokesman. "We felt that was public information."[2]

Information made public also included such facts as the cost of the chemicals used—about $75—and the fees paid the technician and executioner—$500 each per execution. The New York State procedures even dictate the exact words the security supervisor will speak to the witnesses when the execution is over. "Ladies and gentlemen," the official will say, "the physician in attendance has pronounced the inmate dead at _____ P.M. The execution is complete and the officers will now escort you out of the institution."[3]

Death penalty opponents wince at what they see as the matter-of-fact planning of the death of a helpless human being. According to Amnesty International, "a number of doctors have pointed out that the drugs may not work effectively on diabetics or former drug users, whose veins may be hard to reach (a factor that applies to many prison inmates)."[4] In *Should We Have Capital Punishment*, author JoAnn Bren Guernsey describes two Texas cases where lethal injection executions took more than forty minutes each. There are other such accounts repeated by opponents of the death penalty in support of their argument.

Norman Darwick, executive director of the International Association of Chiefs of Police, sees it differently. "Lurid descriptions of the death scene have painted a horrible picture of execution," he grants. "Of equal impact, though," he adds, "are descriptions of the savage atrocities visited upon innocent victims by those who commit murders and rapes. A description of the execution scene which revolts and repels is no more valid a basis upon which to make a decision than is the gore of the criminal homicide scene."[5]

Nevertheless it is a fact that, as the world has progressed, each new means of execution has been introduced with the intention of making it more humane. Neatness also has counted. As humanity has moved away from the idea of suffering being part of punishment by death and towards quicker and more painless executions, it has also sought a *clean* death for the offender.

Brutal Death

This was not always so. A quick, merciful, and neat death is a relatively new idea in human history. In earlier times, as the eighteenth-century Scotch poet Robert Burns put

93

it, "man's inhumanity to man" made "countless thousands mourn!"[6] Executions in different places around the world were most often public spectacles meant to discourage those watching from committing crimes, satisfy the desire for revenge against those who committed them, or simply to entertain. To serve these purposes, there had to be suffering and they had to take time.

History records that "in imperial Rome, crucifixion—nailing offenders to crosses and leaving them to die—was commonly employed for thieves and slaves . . . as was being fed to the wild animals in the Colosseum. Crucifixion was also used in Japan,"[7] where the cutting off of a criminal's head by either the headsman's sword or ax was likewise a common punishment. China too beheaded criminals, as did India.

In South America and parts of Africa, the knife and spear were used to slowly carve up the live victim. According to the *Encyclopedia Britannica:*

> In medieval Europe, hanging was used for offenders of low status and decapitation (beheading) reserved for persons of quality. Heretics were burned, as were witches. In England the penalty of hanging, drawing and quartering was especially brutal. . . . In France traitors were dispatched either by being pulled apart by draft horses, or by being broken upon a large wheel to which they were attached.[8]

In the various navies of the world, up until modern times, seamen were executed for a variety of crimes ranging from mutiny to stealing food. Culprits might be whipped to death or forced to walk a plank at sword-point

Throughout history, an axe and block or a sword were often used to behead criminals.

and jump into the sea to drown. A particularly dreadful punishment was keel-hauling—a practice by which the offender would be pulled by rope or chain under the bottom of the ship and up the other side as many times as it took to finish him.

The horror of such executions became increasingly offensive as various civilizations developed. A belief arose that drawn-out executions brutalized society as a whole, and those who watched them in particular. In eighteenth-century Europe, such influential writers and philosophers as Cesare Beccaria in Italy and Jeremy Bentham in England pointed out that "the ineffectiveness of savage penal laws was self-evident" and that "excessive punishment might be counter-productive."[9] Their point was that a thief who knew that if he was caught he would die by slow torture for his crime, would surely not hesitate to kill. After all, what worse could be done to him?

The Guillotine

Throughout the eighteenth century in Europe, executions became less savage. But the first real move to make the instruments used to perform them more humane only occurred at the end of the century, on April 25, 1792. That was the day the guillotine was first used to execute a highwayman.

A French physician, Joseph-Ignace Guillotin, had become upset by the botched executions he had seen. He had watched hanged peasants slowly choke to death. He had seen the beheadings of nobles painfully botched.

And so he had devised an instrument that would—he thought—end life quickly and painlessly.

This was the time of the French Revolution, and Dr. Guillotin had been elected to the National Assembly (similar to our Congress) in 1789. He succeeded in having a law passed that said that all executions had to be performed by "means of a machine."[10] This meant that ordinary criminals as well as noble offenders would all be executed in the same quick and efficient way—by guillotine.

The device consisted of two upright posts with a crossbeam at the top. A heavily weighted blade was attached to the crossbeam and the insides of the posts were grooved to guide the blade when it was released. A board across the bottom was cut out to firmly hold and support the neck of the one to be executed. A basket was placed beneath it to catch the severed head.

Shortly after the guillotine was introduced, the revolution sank into the Reign of Terror—a bloody period of mounting executions for the most trivial of reasons. Grudges were settled, political rivals eliminated, arguments decided—all by means of the guillotine. But as it was used—as often as twenty, thirty, forty times a day—the executions became less efficient, less neat, less swift, and much less humane.

The constant fall of the blade shifted the weight so that it did not strike accurately. The grooves guiding it wore down with use so that it wobbled as it descended, and as it struck. Sometimes, because of the numbers, the executions were rushed. Sometimes those in charge of them were weary or drunk, and the kneeling person

The guillotine was invented in France as a quick and efficient way to put criminals to death.

awaiting the blade had not been positioned accurately or firmly. Dying took a long time; death was painful.

The guillotine was never used in the United States. (However, a toy guillotine did cross the ocean and proved as popular with American children as with French.) Throughout the eighteenth century and most of the nineteenth, most executions in this country were either done by hanging or firing squad.

"Half-Hanged Maggie"

Hangings were—and are—a particularly painful and not always sure means of putting a person to death. In 1728, an executed woman "woke up in her coffin after supposedly being hung by the neck until dead."[11] To this day she is known as "Half-Hanged Maggie."[12] Her story is not the only one to give hanging a bad name.

In 1901, the outlaw Black Jack Ketchum was hanged in New Mexico. As the drawstring of the hood over his face was tightened, he yelled out "Let her rip!"[13] and that is what happened. When the trap was sprung, the noose tightened, and the rope snapped with such force that Ketchum's head was pulled from his body. There was a similar result in West Virginia in the 1930s when Frank Meyer was hanged for murdering his wife.

Many who are hanged strangle to death slowly, some taking as long as fifteen minutes to die. Sometimes the neck is broken and the person is knocked unconscious, but sometimes that does not happen and there is awareness all during the slow process. Former San Quentin Warden Clinton Duffy who witnessed sixty hangings has testified that most were "of the less than clean variety."[14]

Hanging was a common, but often painful and slow, way to be executed.

Most death penalty supporters do not favor hanging as a method of execution. A few, however, claim that "its very repulsiveness makes it more of a deterrent."[15] Some favor public hangings, and some go beyond that to recommend televising them—as well as other forms of execution—in order to discourage potential murderers.

Presently only four states—Montana, New Hampshire, Washington, and Delaware—have laws that allow executions by hanging. All four, however, also offer alternative methods of execution. In Delaware, if lethal injection is found unconstitutional, then the offender may be hanged. Only two people have been legally hanged in this country since 1976.

Firing Squads

Only one person—Gary Gilmore—has been executed by firing squad since 1976, although this method is legal in Utah and Idaho. Both states also offer alternatives. *The Encyclopedia of American Crime* points out that "in some respects, death by firing squad is the most 'humane' method of all"[16] because it is over quickly. Up until the twentieth century, most condemned prisoners, given the choice, selected it over hanging, which was usually the only other alternative.

There are, however, two reasons why firing squads are rare today. The first is that when they work as they are supposed to, the results are extremely bloody. The sight goes against the trend of "tidy" executions.

The second reason has to do with the method itself. In firing squad executions the condemned person is strapped into a chair in front of a wall with a bright cloth target pinned over his or her heart and a hood over his or her face. Five sharpshooters using .30 caliber rifles are stationed behind an upright canvass sheet twenty feet from their target. Four of the guns are loaded with a single bullet, the fifth with a blank. This is so that sharpshooters can tell themselves that they did not fire the fatal shot. At a given signal they push their rifles through a slit in the canvass and all shoot together.

Sometimes, however, a sharpshooter aims *off-heart* so that while the bullet will strike the person, it will not be the one that kills. In 1951, when Elisio J. Mares was executed by firing squad, all four bullets hit the right side of his chest and he bled to death slowly. In military executions an officer would then have fired a bullet through the brain, the so-called *coup-de-grace*, but this does not happen in state executions.

The Electric Chair

Because shootings and hangings were so dreadful, and because the stories from France of guillotine horrors had been widespread, the electric chair was welcomed when it was introduced in 1890. Indeed, the United States Supreme Court itself said that it would "produce instantaneous and therefore painless death."[17] But a reporter who witnessed the first execution in New York's Auburn Prison described "an odor of burning flesh" and "a blue flame [which] played about the base of the victim's spine." It took over four agonizing minutes to kill him.[18]

The procedure has not really improved over the past hundred years. On May 4, 1990, "it took three separate

2,000-volt surges to kill a man, Jesse Tafero, in Florida. Fire, smoke, and sparks spewed from his head."[19] After reviewing medical evidence and witnesses' accounts of electrocutions, Supreme Court Justice William F. Brennan concluded that the method causes "unspeakable pain and suffering."[20]

The Gas Chamber

Like the electric chair, the gas chamber was introduced to make death easier. It too, however, has drawbacks. They were illustrated by the most famous gas chamber of all, the one built in California's San Quentin penitentiary in 1938.

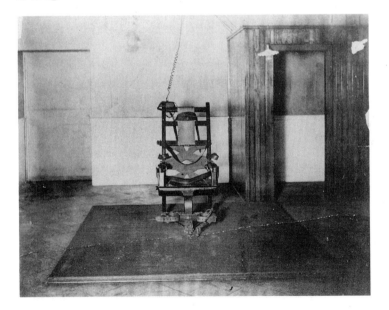

The electric chair is still used in some states as a means of execution.

The way it worked was that the condemned person was strapped into a chair in the gas chamber. Under the chair were shallow pans with tubes leading to them through the walls. A mixture of water and sulfuric acid were fed into the pans. From outside the chamber a lever was pulled and sixteen one-ounce cyanide pellets were dropped into the mixture. Immediately deadly fumes began to rise. They were supposed to cause death quickly.

They often did not. The inmate had been warned that when the odor of rotten eggs was smelled, he or she should count to ten and inhale quickly and deeply. The problem was that the fumes made the victim choke and the normal reaction then was to fight the gas. A witness to the execution of Caryl Chessman in 1960 described what happened after he fought the gas until his head fell forward and his tongue hung out: "I thought he must be dead," she wrote, "but no, there was another agonizing period during which he choked on the gas. And again. And then again." She went on to describe sobs, extreme trembling and the blood draining from his face until finally "I knew he was dead."[21]

The 1983 death by gas of Jimmy Lee Gray in Mississippi was no more peaceful. It took him eight minutes to die. During that time he thrashed about and repeatedly hit his head on a pole behind him.

Doctor Death

There are drugs that might make executions less painful. However, the law requires that the condemned person be fully aware at the time of execution, and so they are not officially used. (Sometimes, though, they are used unofficially.) There is also the problem of who should prescribe and administer the drugs. Doctors are forbidden to by the American Medical Association, which has stated that "a physician, as a member of a profession dedicated to the preservation of life . . . should not be a participant in a legally authorized execution."[22]

The law, however, requires that a doctor be on hand at all executions to pronounce death. Sometimes such doctors perform other tasks such as monitoring the prisoner's heartbeat, advising on dosages of lethal injections, or even helping to keep the prisoner calm. The identity of doctors who take part in executions in any way is always kept secret.

Doctors are undoubtedly as divided in their feelings about the death penalty as other people are. Executions may not be pretty, but neither is murder or rape or other crimes of violence. Those physicians who favor the death penalty believe they are being humane when they cooperate with the state in trying to make death as quick and easy as possible. They point out that their presence guarantees that unnecessary anguish will be avoided. It is not an easy judgment.

Nor is it for the rest of us.

Life and Death: Where and How:
October, 1995[23]

State	Method(s) as of December 1994
Alabama	Electric Chair
Alaska	No death penalty
Arizona	Lethal injection (choice of gas chamber for those sentenced before January 1, 1993)
Arkansas	Lethal injection (choice of electric chair for those sentenced before March 4, 1983)
California	Lethal injection (constitutionality of gas chamber is in the courts)
Colorado	Lethal injection
Connecticut	Electric chair
Delaware	Lethal injection (choice of hanging for those sentenced before June 13, 1986)
Florida	Electric chair
Hawaii	No death penalty
Idaho	Firing squad or lethal injection
Illinois	Lethal injection
Indiana	Electric chair
Iowa	No death penalty
Kansas	Lethal injection (only for those convicted after July 1, 1994)
Kentucky	Electric chair
Louisiana	Lethal injection
Maine	No death penalty
Maryland	Lethal injection or gas chamber
Massachusetts	No death penalty
Michigan	No death penalty
Minnesota	No death penalty
Mississippi	Gas chamber (choice of lethal injection for those sentenced after 1984)
Missouri	Lethal injection

State	Method(s) as of December 1994
Montana	Hanging or lethal injection
Nebraska	Electric chair
Nevada	Lethal injection
New Hampshire	Lethal injection
New Jersey	Lethal injection
New Mexico	Lethal injection
New York	Lethal injection
North Carolina	Gas chamber or lethal injection
Ohio	Electric chair or lethal injection
Oklahoma	Lethal injection
Oregon	Lethal injection
Pennsylvania	Lethal injection
Rhode Island	No death penalty
South Carolina	Electric chair, or lethal injection
South Dakota	Lethal injection
Tennessee	Electric chair
Texas	Lethal injection
Utah	Firing squad or lethal injection
Vermont	No death penalty
Virginia	Lethal injection
Washington	Hanging or lethal injection
West Virginia	No death penalty
Wisconsin	No death penalty
Wyoming	Lethal injection

Also

District of Columbia	No death penalty
Puerto Rico	No death penalty
Federal Government	Method determined by state in which person is convicted
United States Military	Lethal injection

9

Afterword

When United States Supreme Court Justice Harry Blackmun, who had once voted to uphold the death penalty, changed his mind, he said that it was because he felt "obligated simply to concede that the death penalty experiment has failed."[1] On the other hand, his colleague on the Court, Justice Potter Stewart, thought that the death penalty was "suitable to the most extreme of crimes."[2] Who is right?

Perhaps they both are. It is possible that the death penalty fits the crime and at the same time fails to serve its purpose. But what is that purpose? Deterrence? Punishment? A combination of the two? This is only one of the arguments that runs beneath the surface of debates about the death penalty.

Capital punishment, like all matters of public policy, involves deeper questions than those raised in the heat of argument by supporters on both sides of the issue. For example, what do we mean when we say that we hold human life sacred? Do we mean that the deliberate taking of a life is so awful that only the death of the murderer can insure our continued reverence for life? Is that the deeper meaning of *an eye for an eye*? When someone "gets away with murder," does that increase the risk of being killed for all of us? Or is it just the opposite? Does holding human life sacred really mean that never—under any circumstances—shall it be taken away? Does it mean that execution is really a crime of murder committed by the state that denies the sacred nature of life? Do executions weaken the reverence for life? And when that happens, are not the criminals and the weak more likely to kill? Are we not all then more at risk?

There is also the question of the idea of punishment itself. Dr. Benjamin Rush viewed all crime as illness. Those who were ill had to be locked away from those who were not. The aim, which we call rehabilitation, was to cure criminals, not to punish them. He did not believe in executing murderers; he believed in isolating them to protect society, and in making them better when possible.

Two Kinds of Conscience

The problem with this for supporters of capital punishment—aside from the risk of murderers killing again—is that it relieves the killer of responsibility for his deed. This, they say, strikes at the very heart of a civilized society. If the individual is not held responsible for what he or she does, then how can any laws be enforced? If one is not responsible for killing the first time, why not kill again? By this logic, the contract killer and the serial murderer have no more responsibility for the deaths they cause than their victims do. When conscience is abolished, life is indeed cheap.

But it is conscience that stirs those against the death penalty to action. It will not let them stand idly by while their government kills in their name. They believe that by turning technicians into executioners, the state has made them murderers for pay. Innocent people in need of money are turned into hired killers. The taxes that pay them are blood money.

On the contrary, say capital punishment supporters, we are all being unfairly taxed to pay for keeping murderers alive and healthy. When they kill again, it will be our taxes that bought the murder. If we put these murderers to death, we not only save the money—we save lives.

The arguments continue on the surface and beneath it. Does capital punishment take lives or save lives? Is executing an innocent person a worthwhile price to pay for preventing future murders by executing the guilty? Do blacks and poor people commit more murders, or are they victims of a capital punishment system that favors those who are white and wealthy?

Which is the more cruel and unusual punishment: putting a person to death or life imprisonment without parole? Should the death penalty be eliminated or should it be standardized so that it is administered equally in all states?

Should statements by survivors of murder victims be allowed to influence sentencing? Should statements by

An opponent of the death penalty protests in front of a governor's office.

the killer's family, or loved ones be allowed to influence appeals boards to change a sentence from death to a lesser punishment? Shall the appeals process be shortened so that sentences can be carried out more swiftly, or does this deny the condemned the legal right to present reasons why his sentence should be reduced? Should the death penalty be extended to apply to drug crimes and terrorism? Is capital punishment the mark of a civilization dealing with crime or of one that is being inhuman?

Strangers Killing Strangers

Public opinion is constantly shifting. In the 1960s and 1970s the majority of Americans were against capital punishment. Today the majority favor it. In both cases the courts and the legislatures followed along. The question is: What will public opinion be tomorrow?

Two recent developments will affect that opinion. The first is the change in who is most likely to be the victim of a murder. Up until recently, most victims were killed by someone they knew. Family violence, quarrels between neighbors or business partners, crimes of passion, explosions of jealousy—the majority of murders could be traced to causes such as these. But that is no longer true.

According to the Department of Justice/FBI *Uniform Crime Reports* assessment of December 4, 1994, "Every American now has a realistic chance of murder victimization in view of the random nature the crime has assumed. . . . A majority of the Nation's murder victims are now killed by strangers or unknown persons."[3]

More Young Murderers

The second development has to do with the alarming increase in the number of murders committed by young people. James Alan Fox, dean of the College of Criminal Justice at Northeastern University in Boston, broke down the FBI statistics for 1994 and uncovered a "grim truth."[4] Between 1985 and 1993, "the homicide rate among 18-to-24-year-olds jumped 65 percent and among 14-to-17-year-olds it soared 165 percent."[5] What makes this even more alarming is that "the number of young people in the United States will climb sharply in the next few years, with 23 percent more teen-agers by 2005."[6]

Today's young people—you who are reading this—will be adults by then. Hopefully you will inherit a world with a murder rate that will have continued to decline, as it is declining overall today. Nevertheless, it will be a world with more casual killings committed by those the same age as you are now.

How will you punish them? Will it be a life for a life? Or will you abolish capital punishment? The decision will be yours. The time to start thinking about it is now.

Chronology

1692—Salem witchcraft trials are held; twenty people are executed.

1790—American prison system is founded with the opening of Walnut Street Jail in Philadelphia, Pennsylvania.

1845—American Society for the Abolition of Capital Punishment is founded.

1846—Michigan Territory abolishes the death penalty.

1852—Rhode Island outlaws hanging.

1917—Nine states plus Puerto Rico outlaw capital punishment. Five states restore it by 1921.

1927—American League to Abolish Capital Punishment is founded.

1957—Alaska and Hawaii abolish the death penalty.

1958—Delaware abolishes the death penalty.

1961—Delaware restores the death penalty.

1967—Suits brought by anti-capital punishment groups result in a ten-year halt in executions.

1968—In *Witherspoon* v. *Illinois*, the Supreme Court decides that people against the death penalty cannot be kept off juries.

1972—In *Furman* v. *Georgia*, the Court invalidates the death penalty "as administered." Death penalty states scramble to rewrite their laws.

1976—Supreme Court restores the legality of capital punishment when it decides *Gregg* v. *Georgia.*

1977—Utah ends Gary Gilmore's life by firing squad after ten years of no executions in the United States.

1988—Supreme Court rules in *Thompson* v. *Oklahoma* that minors may be put to death.

1989—In *Penry* v. *Lynaugh,* the Court rules that those with low IQs may be executed.

1995—New York restores the death penalty thirty-two years after the last execution; Texas has its one hundredth execution since the death penalty was restored in 1976, also marking the three hundredth person in the nation to be put to death since then.

Chapter Notes

Chapter 1

1. Lewis D. Eigen, and Jonathan P. Siegel, eds., *The Macmillan Dictionary of Political Quotations* (New York: Macmillan, 1993), p. 61.

2. Ibid.

3. *The New York Times*, March 8, 1995, p. A1.

4. Lori Shell, "The Final Moments of Thomas Grasso," *New York Daily News*, March 21, 1995, p. 19.

5. Paul Schwartzman, "Long Day's Deathwatch," *New York Daily News*, March 21, 1995, p. 19.

6. Ibid.

Chapter 2

1. *Encyclopedia Britannica*, Book 8 (Chicago: Encyclopedia Britannica Inc., 1984), p. 807.

2. *The Holy Bible*, King James Version (New York: Oxford University Press, Undated), *Exodus*, Chapter 22, Verse 18.

3. Carl Sifakis, *The Encyclopedia of American Crime* (New York: Facts on File, 1982), p. 638.

4. *Encyclopedia Britannica*, Book 16 (Chicago: Encyclopedia Britannica Inc., 1984), p. 31.

5. Mark A. Siegel, Donna R. Plesser, and Nancy R. Jacobs, eds., *Capital Punishment: Cruel and Unusual* (Plano, Tex.: Information Aids, 1986), p. 2.

6. *The Holy Bible, Exodus*, Chapter 20, Verse 13.

7. Samuel Hand, "The Most Powerful Deterrent," *The North American Review*, December 1881, p. 1.

8. John Stuart Mill, "Society Must Retain the Death Penalty for Murder, 1868," *Three Centuries of Debate on the Death Penalty* (St. Paul, Minn.: Greenhaven Press, Inc., 1986), p. 29.

9. Robert Rantoul, Jr., "Report to the Legislature, 1836," *Three Centuries of Debate on the Death Penalty*, p. 39.

10. Horace Greeley, "The Death Penalty is State-Sanctioned Murder, 1872," *Three Centuries of Debate on the Death Penalty*, p. 38.

11. Ibid.

12. Ibid.

13. Ibid.

14. Ibid., p. 39.

15. William Randolph Hearst, "Punishment No Cure for Crime," *The Congressional Digest*, August-September 1927.

16. Clarence Darrow, "Capital Punishment Will Not Safeguard Society, 1928," *Three Centuries of Debate on the Death Penalty*, p. 50.

17. Robert E. Crowe, "Capital Punishment is a Safeguard for Society, 1925," *Three Centuries of Debate on the Death Penalty*, p. 44.

18. Editorial, *Cleveland Plain Dealer*, January 25, 1925.

19. Ibid.

20. Ibid.

21. *The Death Penalty List of Abolitionist and Retentionist Countries* (New York: Amnesty International, December 1994), p. 6.

22. Ibid., pp. 2, 7.

23. Ibid., p. 4.

Chapter 3

1. Barret Russell, dir., *The Death Penalty* (Albany: State Research Service; Issues in Focus, January 2, 1992), p. 3.

2. Governor's Program Bill Memorandum (Albany: New York State Senate, 1995), p. 1.

3. Mark A. Siegel, Donna R. Plesser, and Nancy R. Jacobs, eds., *Capital Punishment: Cruel and Unusual* (Plano, Tex.: Information Aids, 1986), p. 63.

4. *Crime in the United States: 1993* (Washington, D.C.: U.S. Department of Justice/FBI Uniform Crime Reports, December 4, 1994), p. 283.

5. Ibid., p. 11.

6. *The New York Times,* May 23, 1995, p. A14. (Quoting FBI Uniform Crime Reports update.)

7. Dale M. Volker, *Chronology of Death Penalty* (Albany: New York State Senate, May 1994), p. 4.

8. Ibid.

9. Siegel, Plesser, and Jacobs, p. 63.

10. Edward I. Koch, "Death and Justice," *New Republic,* April 15, 1985, p. 13.

11. Carol Wekesser, ed., *The Death Penalty: Opposing Viewpoints* (San Diego: Greenhaven Press, 1991), p. 58.

12. Ibid., p. 59.

13. Siegel, Plesser, and Jacobs, p. 62.

14. Ibid., p. 61.

15. David Margolick, "25 Wrongfully Executed in U.S. Study Finds," *The New York Times,* November 14, 1985, p. A19.

16. JoAnn Bren Guernsey, *Should We Have Capital Punishment?* (Minneapolis: Lerner Publications Company, 1993), p. 75.

17. Wekesser, p. 151.

18. Siegel, Plesser, and Jacobs, pp. IA, 66.

19. Ibid., p. 65.

20. Ibid.

21. Ibid., p. 66.

22. *The New York Times,* August 11, 1995, p. B16.

23. Ibid.

24. Russell, p. 5.

25. Helen Prejean, C.S.J., *Dead Man Walking: An Eyewitness Account of the Death Penalty in the United States* (New York: Random House, 1993), p. 168.

26. *Death Penalty Fact Sheet* (New York: Amnesty International, October 5, 1995), p. 2.

Chapter 4

1. *USA: THE DEATH PENALTY: BRIEFING* (Amnesty International, 1987), p. 18.

2. Helen Prejean, C.S.J., *Dead Man Walking: An Eyewitness Account of the Death Penalty in the United States* (New York: Random House, 1993), p. 110.

3. *ACLU Fact Sheet: Innocence and the Death Penalty* (Washington, D.C.: American Civil Liberties Union, July 1995), p. 1.

4. Lois G. Forer, *Money and Justice: Who Owns the Courts?* (New York: Norton, 1984), p. 9.

5. *USA: THE DEATH PENALTY: BRIEFING*, p. 4.

6. Ibid.

7. Mark A. Siegel, Donna R. Plesser, and Nancy R. Jacobs, eds., *Capital Punishment: Cruel and Unusual* (Plano, Tex.: Information Aids, 1986), p. 68.

8. Prejean, p. 49.

9. Siegel, Plesser, and Jacobs, pp. 66–67.

10. *USA: THE DEATH PENALTY: BRIEFING*, p. 19.

11. *The Bill of Rights of the Constitution of the United States, Article VIII. Encyclopedia Britannica*, Book 10 (Chicago: Encyclopedia Britannica Inc., 1984), p. 1045.

Chapter 5

1. Elder Witt, ed., *The Supreme Court and Individual Rights* (Washington, D.C.: Congressional Quarterly, Inc., 1980), p. 205 (quoted from *Louisiana ex rel. Francis* v. *Resweber*, 1947).

2. *The Bill of Rights of the Constitution of the United States, Article VIII. Encyclopedia Britannica*, Book 10, p. 1045.

3. Carl Sifakis, *The Encyclopedia of American Crime* (New York: Facts on File, 1982), p. 121.

4. Witt, p. 206.

5. Ibid. (quoted from *McGautha* v. *California*, 1971).

6. Ibid.

7. Mark A. Siegel, Donna R. Plesser, and Nancy R. Jacobs, eds., *Capital Punishment: Cruel and Unusual* (Plano. Tex.: Information Aids, 1986), p. 4.

8. Peter Irons, and Stephanie Guitton, eds., *May It Please the Court* (New York: The New Press, 1993), p. 230.

9. Ibid., p. 241.

10. Ibid., p. 237.

11. Siegel, Plesser, and Jacobs, pp. 8–9.

12. Elaine Landau, *Teens and the Death Penalty* (Hillside, N.J.: Enslow Publishers, Inc., 1992), p. 63.

13. Ibid.

14. Siegel, Plesser, and Jacobs, p. 56. (quoted from *Resolution 2200 [XXI] Article 6, Section 5, of the United Nations International Covenant on Civil and Political Rights*).

15. *USA: THE DEATH PENALTY: BRIEFING* (Amnesty International, 1987), p. 12.

16. *The New York Times,* August 11, 1995, p. B16.

17. Ibid.

18. Ibid.

19. Ibid.

Chapter 6

1. Tina Rosenberg, "The Deadliest D.A.," *The New York Times,* Magazine Section, July 16, 1995, p. 24.

2. American Civil Liberties Union, *Death Penalty Fact Sheet,* June 1995.

3. Rosenberg, pp. 24, 25.

4. Ibid.

5. Ibid., p. 22.

6. Death Penalty Information Center, *1994 Report.*

7. Rosenberg, p. 23.

8. Ibid., p. 42.

9. *The New York Times,* September 26, 1995, p. B2.

10. Rosenberg, p. 24.

11. *Death Penalty Fact Sheet* (New York: Amnesty International, October 5, 1995), p. 2.

12. Rosenberg, p. 24.

13. *The New York Times,* September 2, 1995, p. 25.

14. Ibid.

Chapter 7

1. *USA: THE DEATH PENALTY: BRIEFING* (Amnesty International, 1987), p. 6.

2. 1995 Memorandum in Opposition (Albany: New Yorkers Against Death Penalty, 1995), p. 2.

3. Governor's Program Bill Memorandum (Albany: New York State Senate, 1995), p. 2.

4. Ibid., p. 1.

5. *The New York Times*, August 11, 1995, p. A1.

6. *The New York Times*, October 3, 1995, p. 19.

7. Ibid.

8. Ibid.

9. Carol Wekesser, ed., *The Death Penalty: Opposing Viewpoints* (San Diego: Greenhaven Press, 1991), p. 175.

10. Ibid., p. 177.

11. Ibid., p. 179.

12. Ibid., p. 180.

13. Ibid.

14. Alphonse D'Amato, *Congressional Record*, vol. 137, no. 9, pt. II, January 14, 1991, daily page: S749.

15. Wekesser, p. 172.

16. *The New York Times*, September 16, 1988, op ed page.

17. Ibid.

18. Mark A. Siegel, Donna R. Plesser, and Nancy R. Jacobs, eds., *Capital Punishment: Cruel and Unusual* (Plano, Tex.: Information Aids, 1986), p. 31.

19. Helen Prejean, C.S.J., *Dead Man Walking: An Eyewitness Account of the Death Penalty in the United States* (New York: Random House, 1993), p. 258.

Chapter 8

1. *New York Daily News*, September 2, 1995, p. 2.

2. *The New York Times*, September 2, 1995, p. 25.

3. Ibid.

4. *USA: THE DEATH PENALTY: BRIEFING* (Amnesty International, 1987), pp. 14–15.

5. Mark A. Siegel, Donna R. Plesser, and Nancy R. Jacobs, eds., *Capital Punishment: Cruel and Unusual* (Plano, Tex.: Information Aids, 1986), p. 63.

6. Robert Burns, *Man Was Made to Mourn* (1786), stanza 7. *Bartlett's Familiar Quotations* (Boston: Little, Brown and Company, 1968), p. 493.

7. *Encyclopedia Britannica*, Book 15 (Chicago: Encyclopedia Britannica Inc., 1984), p. 283.

8. Ibid.

9. Ibid.

10. *Encyclopedia Britannica*, Book 4 (Chicago: Encyclopedia Britannica Inc., 1984), p. 788.

11. Barret, Russell, *The Death Penalty* (Albany: State Research Service; Issues in Focus, January 2, 1992), p. 5.

12. Ibid.

13. Carl Sifakis, *The Encyclopedia of American Crime* (New York: Facts on File, 1982), p. 237.

14. Ibid., p. 236.

15. Ibid.

16. Ibid., p. 237.

17. Helen Prejean, C.S.J., *Dead Man Walking: An Eyewitness Account of the Death Penalty in the United States* (New York: Random House, 1993), p. 18.

18. Ibid.

19. JoAnn Bren Guernsey, *Should We Have Capital Punishment?* (Minneapolis: Lerner Publications Company, 1993), p. 53.

20. *USA: THE DEATH PENALTY: BRIEFING* (Amnesty International, 1987), p. 14.

21. Sifakis, p. 240.

22. Ruling of the *American Medical Association's House of Delegates*, 1980.

23. *Death Penalty Fact Sheet* (New York: Amnesty International, October 5, 1995), p. 4.

Chapter 9

1. *The Economist,* March 5, 1994, p. 26.

2. Peter Irons, and Stephanie Guitton, eds., *May It Please the Court* (New York: The New Press, 1993), p. 240.

3. *Crime in the United States: 1993* (Washington, D.C.: U.S. Department of Justice/FBI Uniform Crime Reports, December 4, 1994), p. 287.

4. *The New York Times,* May 21 1995, p. A14.

5. Ibid.

6. Ibid.

Glossary

amendment—A law added to the Constitution.

appeal—Asking a higher court of law to review a case that has been decided in a lower court.

capital punishment—Legally putting a criminal to death.

clemency—Reducing a sentence or granting freedom to an offender.

Constitution—The seven articles and twenty-two amendments that are the supreme law of the United States.

contract killer—One who murders for pay.

criminal justice system—The entire structure—police, prosecutors, defense attorneys, judges, juries, wardens, prison personnel, and executioners—that deals with crime.

crucifixion—Nailing a person to a cross in order to kill him or her.

death penalty—The law that authorizes taking an offender's life.

death penalty resource centers—Federally funded organizations that pursue legal appeals for condemned inmates who have no money.

death row—The prison cell block where condemned prisoners are held until execution.

death sentence—The judgment by a judge or jury that the convicted criminal must die.

defendant—Any person accused of a crime in a court of law.

deterrence—Discouraging or preventing a crime.

electric chair—The apparatus in which a condemned person is strapped, connected to wires, and killed by successive jolts of electricity.

execution—The killing of a criminal authorized by the state.

firing squad—A group of shooters detailed to execute an offender by means of rifle fire.

gas chamber—The room in which the condemned are put to be killed by inhaling poisonous fumes.

guidelines—Rules governing death row and execution procedures.

guillotine—A machine for chopping off heads by dropping a weighted blade.

inmate—Prisoner.

lethal injection—Execution by pumping poisonous chemicals into the bloodstream.

life without parole—Keeping an offender in jail until he or she dies a natural death; an alternative to the death penalty.

lynch—To kill by mob action and without lawful trial.

mitigating circumstances—Conditions or events that may lessen responsibility for a crime.

parole—The release of an offender under conditions which, if not observed, may result in re-imprisonment.

prosecutor—The one who presents the case against the accused in court; usually a district attorney, or a lawyer-member of the district attorney's staff.

retribution—Deserved punishment for evil done.

revenge—Vengeance; retaliation; to get even.

self-defense—To injure or kill in order to keep from being injured or killed.

serial killer—One who murders over and over again.

statute—A law.

unconstitutional—Not in keeping with the laws set down in the United States Constitution, and therefore, not legal.

United States Supreme Court—The highest court in the United States; the court of last appeal; the final judge of what is legal under the Constitution and what is not.

verdict—The decision reached by a jury, judge, or court.

victim—One hurt by a crime.

wrongful execution—The killing of an innocent person by the state.

Further Reading

Guernsey, JoAnn Bren. *Should We Have Capital Punishment?* Minneapolis: Lerner Publications Company, 1993.

Hood, Roger. *The Death Penalty: A World-Wide Perspective.* New York: Oxford University Press, 1989.

Irons, Peter, and Stephanie Guitton. eds. *May It Please the Court.* New York: The New Press, 1993.

Landau, Elaine. *Teens and the Death Penalty.* Hillside, N.J.: Enslow Publishers, Inc., 1992.

Prejean, Helen, C.S.J. *Dead Man Walking: An Eyewitness Account of the Death Penalty in the United States.* New York: Random House, 1993.

Siegel, Mark A., Donna R. Plesser, and Nancy R. Jacobs, eds. *Capital Punishment: Cruel and Unusual.* Plano, Tex.: Information Aids, 1986.

Sifakis, Carl. *The Encyclopedia of American Crime.* New York: Facts on File, 1982.

Wekesser, Carol, ed. *The Death Penalty: Opposing Viewpoints.* San Diego: Greenhaven Press, 1991.

Index

128